D1295873

Elite Women
and the Reform Impulse
in Memphis, 1875–1915

Elite Women
and the Reform Impulse
in Memphis, 1875–1915

Marsha Wedell

Marsha Wedell

The University of Tennessee Press / Knoxville

Library of Congress Cataloging in Publication Data

Wedell, Marsha.
    Elite women and the reform impulse in Memphis,
1875–1915 / Marsha Wedell.— 1st ed.
            p.   cm.
    Includes bibliograpical references and index.
    ISBN 0-87049-704-9 (cloth: alk. paper)
        1. White women —Tennessee — Memphis — Societies and clubs —
History— 19th century. 2. Elite (Social sciences) —Tennessee — Memphis —
History— 19th century. 3. Women social reformers —Tennessee — Memphis —
    History— 19th century
HQ1906.M4W43 1991
305.42'09768'19 — dc20   90-26748
                                                              CIP

For Cynthia and Don —
whose unfailing good humor
keeps us all going

Contents

Illustrations

Elite Women
and the Reform Impulse
in Memphis, 1875–1915

Introduction

Many years ago, I read with great interest Anne Firor Scott's *The Southern Lady*, in which she explained how her investigation into the Progressive Movement in the South kept turning up a woman, or group of women, who played a significant role in reform long before women were enfranchised. This seemed paradoxical to Scott, a southerner herself, who had always "known" that "woman's place" was not in the political arena; and yet, there they were. Scott's work, the seminal study in the history of southern white women, framed many important questions about the role of these women in the South. She dealt with the image of the southern lady, the impact of image on behavior, and how the realities of these women's lives were so often at odds with that image. Scott also answered the criticisms of some male historians, who considered paying so much attention to women a form of female chauvinism, by pointing out that an understanding of the totality of social reality cried out for the addition of women.[1]

Scott's focus on the elite of southern women seemed less a function of conscious choice than a condition of historical circumstance, in that this particular group of women more or less presented themselves. That is, their presence and visibility in the public sphere is what caught the historian's eye. And their visibility, in turn, was largely a function of their elitism, as it gave them the assurance necessary to step out of a woman's traditional role. Thus elite white women became the first "layer" of southern women to be studied.

I became interested in applying Scott's ideas to a particular city. There was a dearth of research on southern women of any sort, and

it seemed that a specific case study would both expand the literature and provide a basis for further generalizations about women's
lives. Memphis became the candidate. It emerged in the nineteenth
century as an important urban area and, late in that century, had
been the birthplace of one of the South's largest women's clubs — the
Nineteenth Century Club. Club women in other parts of the country had significant impact upon their cities, and I wondered about
the influence of a similar group, or perhaps groups, in Memphis.

New research had also come out, offering fresh insight into the
nineteenth-century women's club movement. Karen Blair's *The
Clubwoman as Feminist* had found women's clubs to be important
structures in nourishing sisterhood and providing women a vehicle
of entry into public affairs.[2] Blair's work, however, dealt primarily
with northern and northeastern women's clubs, which were formed
in the early nineteenth century. Other new work, such as Jean Friedman's *The Enclosed Garden*, addressed the question of why the
development of sisterhood in the south had been so much slower
to emerge than in other regions. She pointed out that in the more
rural, tradition-bound South, women's identity was so heavily bound
by family and community rather than by sex, that it was not until
the latter part of the nineteenth century that southern women began to develop a consciousness based on gender and build a support system that would enable them to challenge southern patri-
archal society.[3]

Thus I undertook to explore women's past in Memphis using the
Nineteenth Century Club as a starting point, moving backward
and forward from there in an attempt to discover when a distinct
sense of sisterhood began to emerge, to learn to what extent the
club movement in Memphis was a manifestation of the emergence
of a women's culture, to investigate the nature of that culture, and
to determine to what extent such activity had paved the way for
women's entrance into the political arena. At the very least, these
women had built a public record that had been largely ignored, and
I undertook to investigate and document it. The social scope of the
study to a great degree defined itself, in that the women involved
in these activities were largely elite whites. I found that while they
comprised a small percentage of the total population, they had

exerted a broad influence on the development of the city, as well as in refashioning the standards of genteel behavior.

Women, I discovered, regardless of class or color, had remained a largely ignored component of the city's past. The standard histories of Memphis — when they even mentioned women — depicted them as auxiliaries or adjuncts to some male action, and attention to women's exertions was cast in terms of "giving the ladies their due." In other accounts, women served as handy vignettes and "inserts," presented in isolation from other groups and society as a whole.[4] Or, as was the case in Gerald Capers's *Biography of a River Town*, members of the Nineteenth Century Club were quickly dismissed with the belittling conclusion that their main purpose was merely to enhance the status of their self-made plutocrat husbands.[5] Memphis history suffered not only from the glaring absence of the integration of the female sector of the population into the larger society, but, as one historian has expressed it, from the "tyranny of the foreground actors."[6]

Such treatments had resulted in part because of the nature of traditional history, in which the locus of change was seen to depend upon the male-dominated arenas of public political and economic events, from which women were excluded by law and custom. Women's lack of appearance in these areas, it must be assumed, was taken as an indication of lack of importance. Because of women's absence from the public sphere, there were fewer obvious traces of their past, which discouraged pursuit even further. Little is heard of the women who lived and toiled during the early years of this river city's founding and floundering, since they were not mayors, aldermen, or prominent in the fledgling business affairs of Memphis.

It was not until the early twentieth century, when a number of women in Memphis became involved in the suffrage movement, that any group of women were considered worthy of historical attention; and we do have studies of the suffrage movement in Memphis.[7] Those involved were considered "exceptional women," somewhat removed from the mainstream, and thus worthwhile subjects. If a woman deviated in some way from the prevailing female norms, we are more likely to find something of her movements recorded, as in the case of Frances Wright. Her controversial social experiment at Nashoba, near Memphis, in the early nineteenth century made her indeed singular, and one completely at odds with the prescriptive norms for white, upper-class women of that era.[8]

Only recently have Memphis women been studied within the context of their gender, and their actions integrated into the economy, society, and politics of a particular period. Kathleen Berkeley, with her article on Elizabeth Avery Meriwether, was the first to point to female stirrings in postbellum Memphis.[9] Meriwether was an exceptional woman, but she was also a mainstream elite and a harbinger of changing attitudes. Another article by Berkeley, on women's efforts in 1872 to reform the public schools, also suggested a developing sisterhood.[10] These studies certainly documented that there were women speaking out in public and on public issues.

As my own research was to reveal, there had been a veritable outpouring of organizational and associational activity in Memphis among white, middle-class women, which began in the mid-1870s and continued unabated into the twentieth century. These women had indeed begun to organize, and their activities had significant impact. They adopted a wide range of urban issues as their personal duties, and succeeded in focusing the attention of the community on the appalling living and working conditions of many of the city's residents. Their work in initiating efforts to address such conditions contributed significantly to the eventual recognition by the city of its responsibility to provide municipal welfare and social services for its citizens.

Out of a sense of humanity, prompted by the reforming impulse of an evangelical religious orientation, these women responded to the wretched situations of fellow human beings. They also recognized that such conditions prophesied urban decay, which could act as a brake upon the commercial progress their male equivalents were so confidently predicting for Memphis in the postbellum decades. In the urban mania and capitalistic whirlwind of "getting ahead" in the late nineteenth century, these women exercised a sort of peripheral vision. They called attention to the unpleasant facts of city life, recognizing that there were those who had suffered, not prospered, from America's burgeoning industrial and commercial development. In Memphis, it was largely elite women who responded empathetically to the casualties of capitalism with the suggestion of community responsibility for those hapless ones and their off-spring. In attempting to deal with the problems of the city's poor, the women's actions suggested that Memphis needed to conceive of itself in terms of a totality and to address itself to the development of a sense of community. The basic civic message of white female elites was that Memphis should concentrate on quality of life as well as commercial opportunity—this being the true gauge of a great city.[11] Their activities had an impact upon their male counterparts, who occupied the traditional seats of economic and political power and whose priority was commercial development, in that men found themselves nudged—inch by inch—toward a more rounded vision of the city's needs.

As the women went about their work in the community, they had contact with those from backgrounds different from their own—both white and, to a lesser extent, black. There was recognition of similarity in their lives by virtue of gender, although lines of class and race certainly enforced a distinct distance between them. While the focal point of this work is upon white women of elite social standing, they are but one "layer" of the female population. There remains a great need for inquiry into other groups of women if that totality of social reality is to be fully captured. I speak here for a particular segment of southern women, as they struggled to find a public voice and effect change in their own lives and in their community. But there are many others who can be identified by virtue of race, class, or perhaps ethnic background and whose function in our past remains clouded or unknown but nonetheless vital. The trend in historical research today is in the direction of a multi-dimensional approach, and this work is intended as a beginning as far as Memphis women are concerned—an initiatory leap into a female world of much depth and richness.

This study, then, is partially what Gerda Lerner refers to as "con-tribution history,"[12] in that a fuller account of the beginning of a significant public record for Memphis women seems long overdue, and to record it is to do simple historical justice. However, perhaps more important is the attempt to evaluate this particular group of women in Memphis history within the context of the structural constraints imposed upon them by gender, which dictated certain options and choices. As has been observed, "Choice can be understood only within the framework of available opportunity."[13] The efforts and accomplishments of these women have been cast aside as insignificant for a number of reasons, not the least of which is that the alterations they brought about were not of revolutionary dimensions. However, when evaluated within the circumstances and historical framework that defined and constricted their lives, the changes they effected were considerable. As Karl Marx commented: "Men make their own history, but they do not make it just as they please; they do not make it under circumstances chosen by themselves, but under circumstances directly encountered, given, and transmitted from the past."[14]

Historical study seems to have reached a point where the issue of gender and sex roles has been recognized, at least to some degree, as a crucial category when considering the nature of historical change.[15] In the past couple of decades we have become much better informed about women's lives and more sensitive to the meanings that this heretofore "silent" segment might yield. To ignore the impact of the "home sentiment" upon the direction of events is to overlook a crucial component in the development of a society's perspective.

It seems essential to recognize that women have a point of view and experience distinguishable from that of men. Considering women's historical role, it is not surprising that they were first to call attention to the circumstances of the poor. As society's nurturers, women had been charged with the role of maintaining family welfare, thus increasing the likelihood of female sensitivity to conditions of family distress. Because women made up the greater percentage of church populations, it was they who were the major recipients of the message of social responsibility from late nineteenth-century churchmen. Although women had been engaged in benevolence for some time in a less public way, the additional message helped legitimate and encourage their expanding activities.

The plethora of new undertakings which engaged these elite women of Memphis in the late nineteenth and early twentieth centuries also indicated change within the city's social structure. The process of creating for themselves a new public image precipitated a quiet revolution in women's lives, and they began to construct a distinct female consciousness and an identifiable and public women's culture. They spent their time in new ways, leaving the confines of their homes frequently and regularly to engage in a variety of activities falling under the rubric of philanthropy. They formed organizations, drew up constitutions and by-laws, applied for and received charters from state authorities, managed money and property, and dealt with legislators and lawyers in drawing up bills and lobbying for their passage. Via their club rooms, literary associations, church groups, temperance societies, and suffrage organizations, Memphis women experienced — largely for the first time — the exhilaration of exclusively female cooperative endeavors in the public sphere and began to forge identities for themselves apart from their families. It was no longer necessary to be silent and remain "behind the scenes," as Victorian prescription dictated. In larger numbers than ever before, women began to exercise public authority and participate in democratic decision making. As Anne F. Scott has commented, "Leaders are indispensable, but to produce a major social change many ordinary people must also be involved."[16] In a seemingly methodical way, these women were gradually expanding the contours of their lives, prescriptively as well as in reality. That is, as their actions began to expand the framework of acceptable opportunities for southern ladies, there was a simultaneous alteration in the definition of proper womanhood.

It is necessary to look at what choices were made by these women on the basis of available alternatives, to assess the impact of their choices on themselves as well as on the city, and to understand how these women attempted consciously or unconsciously to change the availability of their options. The women of this study were vitally connected to their society and — through their collective behavior — to each other in new and special ways. They are, in a sense, being put under a microscope — not to separate them but to illuminate how they were active agents shaping their own lives and how they formed an integral part of that elusive puzzle of the past. These women may not have made headlines, but they were making history. They became, in effect, a formidable force for change, and the telling of their story is long overdue. The end result should yield a clearer and more complete picture of the social reality of late nineteenth- and early twentieth-century Memphis.

1

Beginnings of a Female Network

The roots of the organizational flowering of Memphis women can be traced to the early years of the nineteenth century. Prior to the 1830s there are scattered references to group involvement by Memphis women as "nonmembers" of various flourishing lyceums, to which they were allowed attendance to hear lectures and debates. During the decade of the 1830s and into the Civil War years, women became active organizers on their own behalf.[1] These groups were usually associated with a church or synagogue and addressed a specific problem or crisis on an ad hoc basis. For example, the women of the Presbyterian Church formed a sewing circle in 1839 in order "to liquidate as soon as possible the debts which the church now owes."[2] Fairs and various types of fund raisers organized by women became a fairly common occurrence among Memphis church-women throughout the 1840s and 1850s, and they often raised quite substantial sums of money.[3] Through the efforts of the Female Educational and Missionary Society of Calvary Church in the 1850s a "Mission Church" was opened in north Memphis. The women secured a lot, arranged for a building contract, and raised the necessary funds in order to open the new church. Bishop Otey praised their efforts in this project and spoke of the "enterprise" of these "weak instruments."[4]

The Ladies' Hebrew Benevolent Society was also formed in the 1850s. Its purpose was to alleviate "the suffering and destitute of our faith that continually visit our city," and they adopted the motto "In Union There Is Strength." The women were separate from the congregation, autonomous and self-supporting.[5]

These groups kept a low public profile, with their activities confined to aiding their specific church or the poor of their faith, and there does not appear to have been cooperation among them. Yet in joining with those of similar religious persuasion, women had gone out into the community and raised money, they had built a church, and had taken some responsibility for the poor. They were beginning to do things with other women away from the immediate concerns of their own families. It was largely these religion-oriented societies that provided Memphis women with an established base from which support activities for the Confederacy would be quickly formed.

As one historian has said, the Civil War was fought in the front yard of southern housewives,[6] and Memphis women certainly fit that description. Their dedication and work on behalf of the Confederacy were unflagging while holding their families together in the face of constant danger and hardship. Throughout 1861 local newspapers were filled with notices of ladies' church societies announcing the formation of groups to sew on behalf of the Confederacy—uniforms, tents and all manner of necessary supplies.[7] All Memphis women were invited to join the groups regardless of their religious affiliation.

Probably the most widely known of the Memphis women's organizations was the Southern Mothers, begun by Mary E. Pope, who had been very active in Calvary Episcopal Church.[8] Pope published an appeal to "The Women of the South" in April 1861, urging them to form groups to take care of the sick and wounded soldiers. "Let the women of the entire South join and spread the organization till not a spot within the southern borders shall be without its band of sisters, pledged to the work and ready for it."[9]

The response was immediate, and within a week of Pope's letter the Southern Mothers was formed. They explained its purpose was specifically not to "supersede or interfere" with other associations working for the Confederacy, "but . . . to concern itself wholly with the sick and wounded soldiers."[10] Within a few months, the wounded began to arrive and makeshift hospitals were set up in various locations. There was an unceasing flow of soldiers, and after Shiloh, federals came as well. One woman commented upon being "so fatigued that I could scarcely work; yet duty urged me forward, and kept me moving. Sleep was almost a stranger to me for weeks at a time."[11]

While the city's surrender to Union forces early in the conflict, on June 2, 1862, spared much potential physical devastation, Civil War Memphis suffered from overpopulation, social fragmentation, confusion over municipal authority, and physical deterioration. J. M. Keating described the experiences of Memphians during the federal occupation as "bitter beyond belief, and the humiliations put upon her citizens were some of them as brutal as they were causeless and wanton."[12]

Memphis women emerged from these years of hardship and severe deprivation with a sense of pride in their contribution to the Confederacy. They had nursed, smuggled, sewed, farmed, managed property and business affairs, and performed a myriad of crucial civilian support roles. Their ability to cope with the emergencies caused by war demonstrated their competence and capacity for independence and personal autonomy, not only to the public but to themselves as well. They had managed without male help or protection and survived. And many faced the necessity of continuing to cope more or less alone.

Wartime work had invited female participation in a public, civic cause and had widened their experiences. The war had served as an important unifying force and promoted broader cooperation among Memphis women who otherwise might not have become linked. The wartime societies that had grown from church groups invariably invited all women to join regardless of religious persuasion. Their work in all manner of war support activities had developed resources of inner strength and built a camaraderie that was not discarded once the war ended. There was a strong desire to continue their relationships into the postbellum years, as was the case with so many of the southern women's wartime associations; and "lost cause" societies proliferated. In the case of the Southern Mothers, the women remained together, aiding surviving soldiers and later caring for graves in Elmwood Cemetery.[13] While the objectives of postwar organizations such as the Southern Mothers, the United Daughters of the Confederacy, and the Confederate Memorial Association centered around preserving and honoring the memory of southern soldiers and the Confederacy, they gradually expanded their concern into other civic issues.

It seems ironic that some would find a stepping stone into social and political activism via groups dedicated to the perpetuation of the memory of a culture that had been so confining to women. While these impulses appear to be mutually exclusive, their connection might be better understood if considered in the light of women attempting to reconcile their tradition-bound southern culture — which had been their life matrix — with a new role for themselves. The patriarchy, whose authority was already damaged by the Civil War and the loss of slavery, was of no mind to entertain the additional threats to the hierarchy that a widened role for women would certainly bring. Yet for women, the time was ripe for change. Revering the South in their writings, rhetoric, and through their numerous "lost cause" associations provided reassuring evidence of female loyalty to the antebellum world, while allowing them the latitude to make role adjustments. Thus, they could effect change without casting themselves in a radical position. Women could justify public action emanating from a Confederate memorial association in much the same way as activities which sprang from church groups. Such established and acceptable vehicles as doing God's work in the world or glorifying the Old South permitted mainstream entry into public activities and allowed expansion of female authority and responsibility in a manner that seemed compatible with their past.

Elizabeth Avery Meriwether provides an interesting individual case. An outspoken advocate of women's rights in postbellum Memphis, as well as nationally, she wrote a number of books glorifying antebellum southern culture and justifying adherence to the "lost cause."[14] There was no one who defended the South more staunchly than Meriwether, yet there was no woman in Memphis who called more vociferously for a liberalized role for women than she. Kathleen Berkeley notes Meriwether's "herculean efforts to reconcile two conflicting images of womanhood, the veneration of southern white women with its pedestal imagery versus the woman's rights activist;" and her "shrewd" exploitation of one as a mechanism for promoting the other.[15] While Meriwether's views concerning change in

Elizabeth Avery Meriwether. An outspoken advocate of women's rights. Elizabeth Meriwether wrote a number of books both glorifying antebellum Southern culture and actively calling for a liberalized role for women. Reproduced from Elizabeth Meriwether, *Recollections of 92 Years, 1824–1916* (Nashville: Tennessee Historical Commission, 1958).

women's roles went beyond the mainstream in Memphis, sometimes leaving many of her peers behind, her ideas and her assertiveness in expressing them were harbingers of things to come.

A changing attitude on the part of Memphis women can be seen
in the school wage controversy which erupted in 1872 to 1873.[16]
The precipitating event was the cutting of women's wages by the
all-male school board while simultaneously raising the wages of
male teachers. The female teachers, backed by women in the community at large, responded indignantly to what they considered a
blatantly unjust act and protested boldly and publicly. The ensuing
dispute, covered closely in the pages of the *Memphis Daily Appeal*[17] spilled over into the controversial area of male-female hierarchy, and the "woman question" was furiously debated. One school
board member, G. W. F. Cook, argued that women outside the
home were "interlopers who usurped the place and function of
men." He charged that women were inferior to men and stated that
"the only thing the women beat the men at was . . . suckling and
nursing babies."[18]

The women disputed the doctrine of female inferiority and coun-
terattacked by criticizing the school board's management. Elizabeth Meriwether, who was instrumental in organizing support for
the women teachers, said the men managers might be well-meaning
but "are by virtue of their sex not competent to preside over children."[19] The women emphasized their role as primary nurturers
and with this wedge began to assert their "natural place" in the
management and running of the school system. As Meriwether
said during the course of the debate, "when men assume to themselves the whole management of schoolroom and school children,
they are plainly usurping the natural place of women; they are
pushing themselves into our peculiar sphere, against which usur-
pation and which impertinent pushing I must ever protest."[20] It was
clear that Memphis women were not going to sit idly by and have
female competence called into question, especially in matters relating to children.

Their heated response was fueled to some degree by economic
factors, in that there were more women in the postbellum era who
worked for wages which had become vital to their survival. School

teaching was a profession to which the "respectable" classes flocked, and elite women in the larger community empathized with those who found themselves for the first time among the employed. The *Memphis Daily Appeal* spoke up repeatedly in favor of the women teachers on the basis of "the simplest sense of justice."[21] There was also present among the female teachers a sense of community based on ties of friendship and family, which in addition to their collective financial plight provided an important source of unity as they formulated their daring response.[22] Women as a group challenged the all-male school board and expressed great confidence in female competence and responsibility. They offered a plan of reorganization and reform which included, among other points, equal representation between men and women on the school board and pay on the basis of merit and experience instead of gender. They also put forward the name of Clara Conway, one of the city's most respected educators, for the position of superintendent of public schools.

While the women ultimately lost their battle with the school board, getting neither Conway as the superintendent nor equal pay with men, the significance of the controversy can hardly be overestimated. It marked a very important step by elite women in the larger community into the public world, adding fuel to a smoldering fire of recognition of their need for participation in civic affairs. Women accepted their role as primary nurturers, but they further asserted that wifehood and motherhood were compatible with civic involvement.

The teachers' wage controversy also served as an important indicator of a developing female consciousness. The sense of community displayed by the women teachers involved the broader female society, and ties and relationships developed among these women that had a crucial impact upon their future life in Memphis. Clara Conway and Jenny Higbee are two individuals who, while primarily associated with the educational community, provided an important bridge to the larger female world and subsequently exercised great influence upon a developing women's culture.

Conway, whose name was proposed for superintendent in 1873, had been a teacher and principal in the public schools for some

Clara Conway. A proponent of higher education and autonomy for women, Clara Conway ran her own private school for girls. A founding member of the Nineteenth Century Club, she exerted influence well beyond the educational community. Reproduced from *Woman's Work in Tennessee* (Memphis: Printed under the auspices of the Tennessee Federation of Women's Clubs by Jones-Briggs Co., 1916).

years and also exerted influence well beyond the educational community. She spent her life battling for progressive ideas in Memphis
and became prominent in women's club and literary circles. Some
years after Conway's death, women continued to testify about her
inspiring leadership: "Today many of the ladies in the movement
for the intellectual, social and moral betterment of the community
are women who caught the fire of their inspiration from the flame
of her ardent spirit."[23]

Her own school, the Clara Conway Institute, which operated in
Memphis from 1877 to 1893, was the embodiment of her dream of
bringing to the city higher education for women. Among her goals
was the hope of founding a school that would prepare women to
be economically independent. Conway's intention was for her institute to be a college-preparatory school, sending graduates to the
best eastern women's colleges. She read a paper before the Southern
Education Association in 1891 urging a southern university for
women, which she hoped could become for the South what Vassar
and Wellesley were for the North.[24] She believed education would
be the great liberator of women, preparing them "to take part in
the work of the world," and showing them the way toward independence. Conway urged women to "go forward and taste the apple,"
and to those who hesitated she said, "The stale, worn-out argument
that higher education detracts from womanliness has lost its force.
. . . Everywhere one sees high bred women in careers. Independence is one of the highest attributes of womanhood."[25]

Although Conway began her school with only three hundred
dollars of borrowed money and one assistant, it was quickly successful. The school was incorporated in 1885, and its trustees included some of the most influential businessmen of the city.[26] By
1888 the Clara Conway Institute had over three hundred young
women enrolled and a faculty of twenty-six, and was known for
its progressive and innovative approach to education. The circumstances of the school's demise in 1893 are somewhat unclear but
appear to have stemmed from conflict between Conway and her
trustees. She was determined to carry out the college-preparatory
idea over the opposition of her financial backers, who noted "too
much ambition on the part of the principal."[27] Her emphasis on

independence for women and insistence in urging graduates to attend progressive eastern colleges may have become too much for the male trustees, despite her efforts to reassure the patriarchy by conceding that women's education should include the "practical skills of housekeeping" and by reminding men that ignorant women made bad wives and mothers. She was fond of quoting George Eliot in saying, "Only an independent woman could give her hand with grace and dignity. . . . She can afford to wait until the king shall come and if he doesn't she can live her life in her own way."[28] This argument for a more carefully constructed family did not win over the trustees. For Conway herself the "king" apparently did not materialize, she being proof of the independent woman's ability to live her life in her own way.[29]

After the closing of her school in 1893, Conway continued her teaching for a few years but on a smaller scale, with only herself as instructor. Her influence upon her students was deep and lasting, prompting one of them to say:

> Once in a generation there is born one who envisions conditions as they should be — a dreamer. Such as this was Clara Conway. . . . To most of us she sat Minerva-like upon a mystic throne — incomparably wise, brilliant and resourceful, impressing upon each one who passed within the space of her influence the importance of her motto, "Neglect not the gift that is within thee," or that other motto she loved so well, "Influence is responsibility."[30]

The latter motto would be adopted by the Nineteenth Century Club, of which Clara Conway was a founding member. To have been among this small group of charter members is ample testimony to the high status she had achieved within the female community, despite her humble origin as an orphaned daughter of impoverished Irish parentage.[31] Conway saw women's clubs as another curcial educational tool that could bring women into intellectual and community pursuits. She believed that clubs would be woman's "winning card," allowing her to become the "exploring woman," who could at last have the means available to cultivate the power of thought and take "control of her faculties."[32] Conway was an active member of the Nineteenth Century Club, keeping civic issues before the women. She arranged an address by Henry George in

1890 on the topic "The Sphere of Women in Politics and the Interests She Takes in Social Problems."[33] Conway was also responsible for bringing the Association for the Advancement of Women to Memphis for its annual convention in 1892, thus exposing local women to some of the most active female reformers in the country.

The role of catalyst seemed to come naturally to Conway, and it did not stop with efforts to urge women to seek widened horizons. She also had some specific concerns about the development of the city; and in 1889 she publicized her ideas in a speech entitled "A Plea for the Other Kind of Progress" at her Institute.[34] While applauding the mercantile prosperity of Memphis, she posed the question, "Do we live by bread alone? . . . Shall we sit with folded hands and see the city of our love grow one-sided in the direction of commerce only."[35] Conway emphasized the necessity of those materially better off giving so that the whole city could be improved for the benefit of everyone. She noted the existence of disease, misery, ignorance, and crime which continued to plague the city and stressed the need to "close the gap between rich and poor which threatens to be the curse of America."[36] Conway urged individuals to focus attention upon aesthetics and the quality of life in Memphis. Her ideas were practically a blueprint for both the Women's Christian Association — which was already engaged in addressing the plight of poor women[37] — and the Nineteenth Century Club, which would organize the following year and tackle many of the issues Conway raised.[38] Her concerns were not so much startlingly new as they were a boost to the growing sentiment for an end to citizen apathy and the need of continuous citizen involvement in the running of the city. The *Memphis Appeal-Avalanche* pointed out that while "spasmodic efforts born of great calamities" had been made, what the city needed was a group of "disinterested citizens" who would devote themselves to civic betterment;[39] and in this rising chorus Conway was a leader.

Jenny Higbee also emerged from the educational community and played an important role in the initial stages of building a female network in Memphis. A contemporary of Conway, Higbee came to Memphis from New Jersey toward the end of the Civil War to live with her physician brother. She had attended a well-known female

Jenny Higbee. A pioneering advocate of higher education for women. Jenny Higbee in 1878 opened her own school for girls in order to prepare graduates for entrance into the best women's colleges. Reproduced from *Woman's Work in Tennessee* (Memphis: Printed under the auspices of the Tennessee Federation of Women's Clubs by Jones-Briggs Co., 1916).

seminary in Moorestown, New Jersey, run by Mary Lippincott, where teachers described Higbee as "a genius."[40] Upon moving to Memphis, she began teaching in the public schools and was principal of the Court Street Female High School at the time the wage controversy erupted. Quite a number of the public school teachers had received their training under Higbee at the Court Street School,[41] and the camaraderie and strong sense of community they displayed in the wage fight was, in all probability, attributable in no small degree to the active role model Higbee provided. Her personality was described as "strong, energetic and progressive,"[42] and her vigorous leadership and dedication to educational pioneering were given high praise: "Taking a stand for the higher education of women when the idea was too new to have gained scarcely more than a foothold, it became the consuming theme of her life."[43]

Higbee opened her own school in 1878 and, like Conway, hoped to prepare graduates for entrance into the best women's colleges. She recruited teachers from the East and opened a boarding department in order to serve surrounding areas as well as Memphis.[44]

On the twenty-fifth anniversary of her work as an educator, women who had attended the different schools in which she had taught formed Higbee Alumnae Association and dedicated themselves to community work. Higbee's influence, via her students, was said to "permeate throughout the entire South. . . . When two or three gather together, her name is nearly always mentioned." Said one, "'She was the strongest influence of my life.'"[45]

Higbee was also among the Nineteenth Century Club's earliest members, though not a charter member, and was closely associated with the social elite of Memphis. She and Clara Conway provide excellent examples of professional women who also occupied elite positions within the social hierarchy of late nineteenth-century Memphis. Such a combination was in itself indicative of change in women's lives, as well as a changing attitude by and about women. Their schools, which inculcated attitudes of independence and autonomy in their students, and which were patronized largely by the elite families of Memphis, also indicated a shifting view of women's future. It was Conway who said that woman's highest duty was to herself and therein lay the key to happiness. "This duty is her highest responsibility," she said, "not her duty to her husband."[46] The atmosphere of encouraging female autonomy and the growing confidence in women's intellectual capacity and competence became pervasive in late nineteenth-century Memphis. The school wage controversy had been enormously important in focusing wide public attention on the "woman question" and in fostering a more liberal view of women in society.

It was also out of the ferment surrounding the wage crisis that the the public careers of the women's rights advocates, Lide and Elizabeth Meriwether, crystallized—illustrating yet another facet of the fallout from this landmark episode. Women's public involvement would come in many shades and in varying degrees, and the Meriwethers, while located more toward the radical end of the female reform spectrum, would also provide role models for an emerging woman's culture. Consumed by the traditional duties of wifehood and motherhood for much of their lives, they became outspoken on a wide range of issues related to woman's position in society, which made them decidedly unusual for aristocratic southern ladies. Yet they were admired and respected by many men and women for the very qualities which differentiated them. The Meriwethers' social rank also insulated them to a great extent from damaging criticism.[47] They were linked by marriage to men who were quite visible in the Taxing District oligarchy, and who supported and encouraged their wives' public activities.[48] Elizabeth Meriwether's husband, Minor, had played an important role in the coup of the land barons who engineered the inauguration of the Taxing District in 1879. Lide Meriwether's spouse, Niles, was city engineer for much of that time. The two families shared a residence in Memphis for a while, and obviously the chemistry was very positive within this family group of civic-oriented, self-propelled individuals.

Elizabeth Meriwether appears to have harbored maverick tendencies since childhood, questioning established views and casting a critical eye on society's sacred cows throughout her life.[49] She explained in her memoirs that "it has not always been possible for my mind to accept the dogmas which good religious men declare should be accepted,"[50] and acknowledged being "disputatious." Expressing doubts about the Christian concepts of predestination and hell, she said:

> It seemed to me preposterous to imagine that a good God would create a human being with the power to feel and to suffer if He knew before creating that being that its fate was Hell for all eternity . . . and so it seemed to me . . . that there was a flaw somewhere in the belief of the people about me . . . and I came then to the opinion I still hold . . . that the Hell we mortals get is of our own making and that we get it on this earth and not in a future life.[51]

Meriwether also attacked sex bias within organized religion, charging priests with introducing and enforcing the concept of male dominance above the early christian doctrine of equality.[52] She rarely hesitated in making her private opinions public, and authority figures — whether in the religious or civil hierarchy — presented no problem to the expression of her sense of justice. Meekness was not among her characteristics, a fact made clear by her Civil War experiences when she found it necessary to fend for herself and young children in the face of severe food shortages, harassment from vagrants, and a period as refugee when she and her children were ordered out of Memphis by the Union commander.[53] Always a fighter and a supremely self-confident woman, Meriwether was not one to sit on the sidelines. For much of her adult life she battled from the speakers' platform and with her pen for equality for women. There was hardly a civic issue where women were concerned that did not engage the participation of Elizabeth Meriwether.

In January 1872, Meriwether began publication of a newspaper, *The Tablet*, which she intended as a vehicle to express and publicize women's issues. She said she fully expected women to become a power in the world and her intention was for *The Tablet* to be their mouthpiece. She wrote in the first issue that although many of "our gentlemen friends have advised against this enterprise . . . every one of our lady friends not only favor it, but are enthusiastic about it.[54] *The Tablet* proved a short-lived forum for Meriwether's ideas on reform, as she found being editor, publisher, and contributor — in addition to family commitments — too much for her health; she sold her paper to a local printing company in June.[55] It was shortly thereafter that Meriwether became involved in the teachers' wage dispute and her thinking on women's rights crystallized in the direction of woman suffrage as the key to female independence.[56] The women lost their fight for wage equality, for Conway as superintendent, and — it seemed to Meriwether — for all the other issues bearing upon female inequality because women were barred from the electoral process. Meriwether subsequently became a member of the National Women's Suffrage Association and in 1876 sent a communication to the National Democratic Convention in St. Louis urging the inclusion of woman suffrage in its platform.[57] She also insisted on casting a ballot in the 1876 presidential election, an action inspired by Susan B. Anthony, whose attempt in 1872 had led to her arrest. No action was taken against Meriwether in Memphis, however, probably because of the family's prominence in the community and the fact that both the judge and the clerk of election in her precinct were her husband's friends. She suspected her ballot was subsequently destroyed.[58] Nevertheless, she was trying to call attention to what she considered the "monstrous injustice, as well as stupidity, of including educated women with felons and lunatics as persons denied the right of suffrage."[59]

It was also in 1876 that Meriwether took the pathbreaking action of renting the Memphis Theater on the night of May 5, to deliver a public address on the topic, "The Spirit of English and American Law as it Relates to Woman."[60] Memphis was rife with speculation over her "debut on the rostrum as a lecturer,[61] because of the public display by a woman of her social standing as well as the nature of her speech. The entire episode, acknowledged the *Memphis Daily Appeal*, had indeed "set the tongue of the town wagging on the woman question."[62] The paper, however, responded very favorably to Meriwether's speech and urged attendance:

> The women of Memphis should, instead of holding back, go forward and encourage her by their presence; especially should all those of them who believe in and are compelled to work be present to hear what she has to say touching the disabilities they are yet compelled to live and labor under. And every man who honestly believes in reform, who desires to see the race advanced in happiness and toward content, should be present to strengthen a citizen who, for the first time, ventures upon an untried path, a path beset with more than ordinary difficulties, and through which she seeks the good of woman. . . . Let us give her a respectful hearing.[63]

Meriwether's lecture was both well attended and well received. Some of her prominent female friends had decorated the stage with flowers, and two of them accompanied her on stage the night of the speech.[64] One distinguished lady friend, Mrs. M. C. Galloway, told Meriwether her speech was "superb," the most interesting lecture heard in Memphis in a long time. Meriwether's husband was described as "gravely contented," and a number of lawyers and judges complimented her "intellectual effort," some of them even coming on stage to congratulate her.[65] Another described Meriwether as "one of Memphis' bright and resplendent intellectual satellites. She is the great orator of the South."[66] The *Memphis Daily Appeal* was also full of praise and urged Meriwether to continue her work.[67]

Such support provides compelling confirmation of approval of Meriwether's ideas and actions, however unusual. While most of her acquaintances neither would have, nor could have, delivered such an address and were not quite ready to follow en masse, Meriwether's public statement had aired, one suspects, many a pent-up sentiment held by the mainstream. She had not feared to say what others had known for some time: that women were intelligent, capable human beings who labored under many handicaps artificially imposed by a wrongheaded society. Meriwether had amply demonstrated intellect in a female, and her speech marked a growing acceptance of a more public persona for women.

While Elizabeth Meriwether left Memphis in 1883 to take up residence in St. Louis, the other half of the female Meriwether equation, Lide, remained and became one of the city's leading temperance workers and elder stateswoman of the local suffrage scene.[68] Equally as self-confident and outspoken as her sister-in-law, Lide also took an active part in the teachers' pay controversy, having come to Memphis as a schoolteacher herself about 1850. Although not as much is known about Lide's early influences, what is known helps to illumine her subsequent role as a women's rights advocate.

Lide Smith was born in Virginia in 1830, shortly after which her mother died. Lide and her sister, Virginia, were sent to Pennsylvania to live with their grandparents, who subsequently sent the girls to the Emma Willard seminary in Washington, Pennsylvania.

Upon graduation, they learned that a debt had been incurred for their education. Determined to repay it, they took teaching jobs in the "wild west," which was Helena, Arkansas, and then Memphis, where Lide met and married Niles Meriwether in 1856.[69]

It took intrepid souls, especially for young women, to embark on such an independent course, a fair indication of the impact of their education as well as the mettle possessed by both, made manifest in their later lives. Virginia's life took a more literary direction and she became a noted southern writer as L. Virginia French,[70] while Lide embarked upon social reform.

That the two women were given an education of the Willard variety, and at apparently some financial sacrifice on the part of their family, is an indication that they were raised in an atmosphere characterized by liberal and enlightened ideas concerning woman's place in society. As Anne F. Scott has argued, Emma Willard's educational innovations were a very important component in the emergence of a new personality type: "the educated woman who was not ashamed of learning and who would inevitably have a wide notion of what the world had to offer her sisters who had not been encouraged to read widely or to think for themselves."[71] Emma Willard's revolutionary ideas on women's education, stressing the need to awaken and develop their intellectual capabilities and imbue students with a seriousness of purpose beyond the domestic and religious spheres, had spread across early nineteenth-century America via graduates who established outposts of the Troy Female Seminary in the Northwest, Southeast, and finally, Southwest.[72]

Elizabeth Meriwether, the elder of the two Meriwether sisters-in-law, had vowed that after her children were raised she would devote her life to "the service of humanity,"[73] and it appears she influenced the development of Lide's opinions. After returning from the National Women's Suffrage Association Convention in 1879, Elizabeth Meriwether claimed Lide and Niles were among the first converts.[74]

Each Meriwether had her last child in 1862, and Lide's life just after the Civil War was described as "a simple home life, devoted to husband and children, to the needs of neighbors, and to personal charities." Then, when "most women are only waiting to die, their

Lide Smith Meriwether. An initiator of several women's issues in Memphis, Lide Meriwether was convinced that women were the initial hope of the country and "should take their rightful place in the world." She was president of the Tennessee WCTU from 1884 to 1897, was active in the work of the WCA, and was an advocate for women's suffrage. Reproduced from Mattie Duncan Beard, *The WCTU in the Volunteer State* (Kingsport, Tenn.: Kingsport Press, Inc., 1962).

children reared and the tasks of the spirit largely ended," she began a "life of larger thought and activity."[75]

While Lide Meriwether's activism became full-fledged only in the 1880s with the Woman's Christian Temperance Union and subsequently with woman suffrage work, her ideas had been germinating for quite some time. In 1872 she attracted public attention with the publication of *Soundings*, a collection of poems and sketches relating to the condition of the "fallen woman," which was a point blank attack on the double standard and hypocrisy of genteel society.[76] She was fully aware of the risky nature of her subject but explained that many friends had urged the book's publication, and — coincident as its appearance was with the controversy swirling around the "woman question" in that same year — the book was no doubt related to that conflict. *Soundings* called attention to the unequal and unjust application of genteel social standards in respect to men and women at a time that the wage dispute illumined the difficulties women encountered in providing themselves adequate financial means. Failure of women to provide for themselves by respectable means, argued Meriwether, could lead to the economic desperation that forced women into prostitution, thus bringing down upon them society's condemnation. Meriwether's outraged sense of justice took public form in the 1870s, a stance from which she never retreated.

Neither of the Meriwether women shrank from fishing in troubled waters. Both expressed themselves freely about the injustices they observed and believed the work they did genuinely furthered human progress. Their willingness to tackle difficult issues in the full glare of the public, while managing to emerge with their respectability intact, must have been an inspiration to those who teetered on that precarious pinnacle of status — struggling on the horns of the difficult dilemma of whether to make a public issue out of their private feelings. Lide, who remained in Memphis throughout her adult life, spent much of her reform career coaxing other women into formulating public stands they knew to be just and right, even though such opinions might challenge convention. At a state Woman's Christian Temperance Union convention in Nashville in 1887 Meriwether said, "whoever hesitates to utter that which she thinks the highest truth, lest it should be too much in advance of the time, must remember that while she is a child of the past, she is also a parent of the future, and her thoughts are children born to her, which she may not carelessly let die."[77] This parent-child metaphor indicates that Meriwether was sensitive to the strictures for women inherent in the postbellum world while she tried simultaneously to lead the way out of that same world.

Throughout the closing decades of the nineteenth century, the collective womanhood of Memphis began to take on the characteristics of the new standard for women developing in nineteenth-century America: the socially concerned woman who was also the good wife and mother.[78] Activism in the pursuit of selflessness and doing their God-ordained work of being mothers to the world would become women's narrow bridge into the public sphere. It was a rather forbidding bridge, as they were, after all, invading the traditional turf of the patriarchy. Ultimately, intellectual and autonomous women could upset a social order based on male supremacy. Nevertheless, Memphis women were beginning to find their public voice and grope for ways to fit themselves into a part of society from which they had been largely separated. The lives of Conway,

Higbee, and the Meriwethers contained incentives for social change, and their sensitive, vital minds, reflected the needs of a larger body of women. They had generated greater confidence in female intellect and brought an infusion of energy to the rising convictions that there were wrongs needing to be set right and that the moment for them to do so had arrived. From the Civil War through the post-bellum years, the female vision was being enlarged, and women began to see the possibilities for shaping society by the extension and application of their intelligence and will. The wage-equity conflict in the Memphis public schools had raised the issue of women's proper place. On the heels of that controversy, and with a pestilential yellow fever epidemic in 1873 which increased the suffering in the lives of many already living marginally, the social concerns of many of the female elite of Memphis coalesced into an organization formed in 1875 dedicated to "the improvement of the moral, social and intellectual condition of women and children"[79] — the Women's Christian Association of Memphis.

2

The Women's Christian Association

The Women's Christian Association was a national organization established in 1869 to address problems faced by women in a newly urban, industrial America. Their purpose, as declared at the first annual meeting, was "the spiritual, moral, mental, social, and physical welfare of women in our midst."[1] Throughout the 1870s, associations of these women began to appear, and in Memphis members took pride in describing their services as being "for the good of women . . . carried on wholly by women."[2] The groups were locally autonomous, selecting their own names and making their own by-laws and conditions of membership.

The Memphis WCA was the brainchild of Elizabeth Fisher Johnson, who became the association's first president, serving until her death in 1883. At her initiative, a small group of Christian women met in April 1875, adopted a constitution, drew up by-laws, and elected officers, thus creating the Women's Christian Association of Memphis. According to their constitution, "Any woman of good moral character, desiring to engage in Christian work, or contribute to the same, may become a member of the Women and Young Women's Christian Association of Memphis, Tennessee."[3] These women took the lead in publicizing the need for improved municipal conditions and insisted that it was the responsibility of private citizens and, ultimately, the city government to take action on behalf of the indigent population, particularly women and children.

Elizabeth Johnson was described as one who was "deeply impressed by the needs of her own community."[4] She was born in 1835 and reared in a family with some experience in public work.

Her father, Major G. W. Fisher, represented Shelby and Fayette Counties in the state senate for several terms prior to the Civil War. He was also a successful and prominent planter.[5] Major Fisher apparently valued education for his daughters, as Elizabeth and a sister, Barbara, attended a girls' boarding school in Macon that was run by teachers trained at Emma Willard schools in New York and South Hadley, Massachusetts.[6]

As in the case of Lide Meriwether, exposure to an Emma Willard-inspired seminary must surely have had some impact upon the outlook and attitudes of Elizabeth Johnson, particularly in view of her subsequent immersion in pioneering philanthropy in Memphis. She certainly fitted the Willard mold of taking charge of the world when it was off track and attempting to set it straight again.[7]

Elizabeth Johnson's religious background was undoubtedly another factor in molding her world view. She was a Presbyterian of deep religious conviction; her daughter said Johnson's life had been "one of complete consecration to the work of Christ."[8] The role of evangelical religion in infusing women with the mission of bringing about the Kingdom of God on earth has been well documented.[9] Evangelical theological tenets, which stressed personal experience and individual worth, had potentially liberating implications for women, easing their movement out of the home and into the public sphere.[10]

Johnson also had some personal contact with Frances Willard, the driving force of the Woman's Christian Temperance Union. Johnson entertained Willard when she visited Memphis in 1881, and her well known dynamism and charisma must surely have affected Johnson, as few who met Willard remained unaffected.[11] Elizabeth Johnson also pioneered in temperance work in Memphis and issued a rather Willard-sounding appeal to Memphis women to "do something, if it is only to gather young girls off the streets to teach them dressmaking, fine mending, cooking, household economy."[12] While Frances Willard urged her followers to "do everything," meaning to involve themselves in every reform effort of the day, Johnson's "do something" was tailored to the Memphis locale and limited, as her comment reveals, to activities of a very domestic nature. Nevertheless, she was taking the first step of coaxing southern women beyond their front doors.

In May 1872, the Johnsons moved from Shelby County to a home on the outskirts of Memphis, where their eighth and last child was born that December.[13] With childbearing behind her and material circumstances affording domestic help, Elizabeth Johnson set out upon what developed into a new career for herself, a career that would have a deep impact upon the Memphis community and the role of women in the city.

The immediate catalyst for initiating the WCA may well have been Johnson's involvement in the Memphis Bethel, a group of men and women whose stated objective was "to encourage and aid the poor in making a living."[14] In 1875 Johnson was president of that group's sewing circle, in which some twenty ladies instructed about fifty "scholars" in the art of handling the needle and shears. It was said that the ladies "also teach by force of example, the way, the truth, and the life." The members of the Memphis Bethel, which was interdenominational, described themselves as being involved in "enlightened liberal Christianity," believing that if the "poor little children" could be practically instructed and educated, they would become productive and responsible members of society.[15] The Memphis Bethel operated a Sunday School and attempted to impart some practical skills, as in the case of Johnson's sewing circle. While the Bethel's board of directors was male,[16] much of the work was carried on by women. They became increasingly aware of situations of family distress stemming from poverty, sin, disease, and ignorance, which cried out to them for attention. Their work in the Bethel presented an ideal opportunity for women to assert themselves and assume a leadership role, and Johnson was quick to capitalize upon it.

"Mrs. Johnson heard the cry of ignorance, want and sin and went to every pastor in the city preparing the way for this movement [WCA]."[17] The WCA became the first organized and concerted effort in Memphis to focus on the special needs of women and children. As the women themselves expressed it: "Whatever affects the physical, moral, mental or spiritual well-being of women properly and naturally falls under the scope of this work and purpose;[18] thus they closely echoed the objectives of the national group. The use of the words *properly* and *naturally* are significant, indi-

Elizabeth Fisher Johnson.
Founder of the Women's
Christian Association, as well
as a main organizer of the
Woman's Christian Temperance
Union in Memphis. She died
at age forty-seven, only six
months after becoming the
first president of the WCTU
for the state of Tennessee.
Reproduced from Mattie
Duncan Beard, *The WCTU
in the Volunteer State*
(Kingsport, Tenn.: Kingsport
Press, Inc., 1962).

cating the growing belief that women should assume responsibility
not only for their own lives, but also for women in the community
at large with whom there was an assumed affinity and natural
understanding based on gender. That which had to do with the
affairs of women and children was increasingly seen by the women
of the WCA as their natural and proper province and responsibility.
The *Memphis Daily Appeal* reported the founding of the WCA by
explaining that the women wanted to "enlarge and systematize the
missionary and benevolent work assigned to ladies, as their legitimate field, bringing together a body of Christian workers from all
denominations who may cordially unite in their labors for the master."[19] The Women's Christian Association marked the beginning
of a municipal housekeeping movement in Memphis, as it extended
the values of the home into the public sphere. Karen Blair in *The
Clubwoman as Feminist* has pointed out that women invoked the
municipal housekeeping idea by insisting that "Women's function,
like charity, begins at home and then, like charity, goes everywhere."[20]
The formation of the WCA in Memphis also indicated a recog-

nition on the part of its organizers that many women were subject
to situations in a nineteenth-century urban setting with which they
could not be expected to cope individually. The WCA members
were aware of the lack of job opportunities for women and low
wages paid to them in available work. They had heard stories of
alcoholism and abandonment and knew the sad plight of many
women left to their own resources — penniless, uneducated and unskilled, often with dependent children. Such people were largely
ignored in a society that emphasized individual responsibility and
had little sympathy for those regarded as "unfit" for life's struggle.
The yellow-fever epidemic of 1873 in Memphis undoubtedly intensified already difficult economic conditions, and, with crop failures
in 1875, the *Memphis Daily Appeal* referred to that year as one of
"unusual difficulty."[21] Out of a dual sense of Christian duty and
sisterly sympathy, the women organized in order to be able to offer
some assistance to those women and children who lived in situations of hopelessness and poverty. While the women of the WCA,
like their husbands, came from stock that paid proper homage to
the nostrums of individualism, and while they could bask con-
tentedly in the material comfort their spouses' financial success provided, their sense of duty spurred them to take up the work of
Christ in this world.[22]

The appeal of the WCA was ecumenical within a Christian context, in that members from all denominations were welcomed and
no religious distinction was made among those they intended to
serve. The word *Christian* was indispensable, they explained, meaning "Christ in the midst,"[23] again echoing the national organization
whose motto was "everything we do is religious."[24] Their board of
managers was composed of two women from each participating
church,[25] and in 1881 the board roster, listed by churches, consisted
of representatives from seven Presbyterian churches, four Methodist churches, two Baptist churches, one Christian church, and one
listing for "Episcopal churches."[26] Of the three women who served
as president of the organization from its beginning in 1875 through
the turn of the century, one was Presbyterian, one Methodist, and
one Episcopalian. Their universal appeal among Christian denom-

inations was considered by the women to be one of their greatest strengths, and they described their work as "interdenominational," insisting "there has never been any discord on this account."[27] During the Civil War, women from various churches had cooperated.[28] Once again identifying a universal need, they saw strength in numbers, this time cemented by the common bond of doing Christ's work in the world. Viewing themselves as agents of unity within the Christian "family" of Memphis, an editorial in *The Gleaner* — a publication of the local WCA — said the organization was

> peculiarly adapted to the needs of smaller cities and towns. The willing and wise-hearted women of a few weak churches may, combined, make their influence potential for the betterment of the world about them as they could not possibly do otherwise. And each woman will be a more useful member of her own church by means of her association, training and development."[29]

The first step of the WCA was to divide the city into districts with a chairman and committee for each. Thus, they began systematic visiting in the homes of the poor in order to acquaint themselves with the actual conditions in which people were living and to ascertain their needs. These visiting committees dispensed food, fuel, clothing, and sometimes cash, as they felt the situation warranted. Missionary work of bringing people to Christ was high on the list. The WCA wanted to bring the adult poor to "God's house" and their children to "sabbath school" in the conviction that religious faith would offer, if not a panacea for problems, at least membership in a community of love "that Jesus meant for all as heirs together in the grace of God."[30] The WCA members believed religious solace might sooth the earthly situations of the poor and hoped that adherence to Christian faith might well lead to a solution of earthly problems.

Almost immediately following the organization's formation, an "Intelligence Office" was opened at 30 Jefferson Street, which served the purpose of finding jobs for women as well as homes for them and their children. It evolved into a general bureau of information about the city's poor. It was to this office that donations of food, clothing, and money were sent, and from which they were dispensed at the direction of the visiting committees. Members of the visiting committees also held weekly meetings at the Intelligence

Office to discuss conditions the members had seen during the week and to determine action to be taken. Through word of mouth and newspaper publicity, Memphians were urged to refer those in need to the WCA's Intelligence Office, enabling the organization's visiting committees to investigate and provide aid "as facts warrant."[31] The poor were generally categorized as "deserving" and "undeserving"—the former being defined as those who made efforts to help themselves, the latter as "professional (or chronic) paupers" who were intent on fleecing residents and who would gamble away or spend on alcohol any money given them.[32] Citizens were urged never to give money to any beggar "without ascertaining the facts,"[33] a task the WCA visitation committees felt they were equipped and willing to do. Such methods, they believed, would help rid Memphis of "beggars and tramps" and avoid "fraud and deception on the part of those simply desiring an eternal handout."[34] As the women approached the problems of urban poverty in late-nineteenth-century Memphis, self-help became the keynote of their solutions, revealing a distinct middle-class bias and orientation.

The WCA's approach was pragmatic in that their activities developed as circumstances dictated and they operated largely on an experimental basis. "God has led us, often not in paths that we would have chosen."[35] Thus, not long after organizing to help poor women in Memphis, the WCA found themselves immersed in the problems of prostitution and homeless children.[36]

Just before the close of the year 1876, the WCA engineered the opening of a Mission Home as a refuge for women who had "fallen from virtue." At their Intelligence Office, the WCA saw many who had come seeking livelihoods but were condemned by their past and automatically shut out by society as "moral lepers." Whatever the members' attitudes may have been before contact with these outcasts, the dilemma they faced was quickly grasped, and the WCA recognized the desperate need for a place to deal sympathetically with those who had turned to prostitution and succumbed to "the grasp of the evil one."[37]

The Memphis WCA opened their home for the moral and social regeneration of "erring women" in December 1876, at the Navy Yard on Promenade Street; it was commonly referred to as the

"Navy Yard Mission."[38] The mission was moved several times through the years, and its focus changed as circumstances required. The Navy Yard Mission, for example, became the Mission Home in 1880 when, due to overcrowding, it was moved to new quarters on Alabama Street. Neighbors objected to the new location, claiming it was a "nuisance" that compromised the "desirability of their neighborhood and value of property." The Grand Jury commended the women on their work but urged relocation "to some more suitable location outside the city limits."[39] In November 1888, the "Magdalens" were moved to a residence on Walker Avenue at Fort Pickering, where the mission work continued under the new name of the Refuge, and the vacated quarters on Alabama Street were turned into the Children's Home.[40]

By the mid-1880s the Mission Home had been averaging from fifty to fifty-five residents, with as many as one-half that number being children. Most of the children had a living parent, which disqualified them from the city's orphanages.[41] Some of them were infants born to residents of the home; some had been brought there by police and private citizens and others by parents who were unable or unwilling to care for them.[42]

The reformers were undaunted by this influx of children and applied their efforts to the problem at hand. A teacher was employed for the children, in whom the WCA hoped to "plant the seed of Christianity."[43] Most seemed to feel the addition of children created a family atmosphere, and they were described as having "a sweet influence upon many otherwise hardened hearts." The Mission Home itself was depicted as "a wayside inn," that furnished "the children home training, nursing, love."[44]

The separation of the women and children in 1888 into the Refuge and Children's Home was probably related to the demands of space, as numbers were increasing and the WCA prided themselves on never having turned away any child. The Children's Home described its purpose as being "to ameliorate and elevate the condition of poor and unfortunate children who are not eligible for orphan asylums and to provide a temporary home for those whose parents are seeking employment. It is not an orphanage . . . it is a refuge, a home for those who in most cases are worse [off] than orphans."[45] The Children's Home became one of the component branches of WCA work with its own board of managers and separate finances.[46]

Work at the Refuge remained an important and ongoing project of the WCA. The major objective was the rescue of women in "soul and body," and a Christian religious emphasis was ever present and regarded as the chief ingredient in the reclamation of these lost souls. The WCA emphasized rehabilitation and pointed out that the law offered nothing but condemnation and prison doors for the "fallen"[47] Permanent reclamation of the "fallen" required that they be equipped with some job skills, the absence of which had been a major factor in bringing on their troubles in the first place. It was here that the WCA seemed least able to break new ground. The constant theme running through reports made by the WCA's Intelligence Office was that requests for household workers was greater than could be filled because of the lack of domestic skills. Thus it was these skills the WCA sought to teach to residents of the Refuge, hoping to prepare them for jobs as competent domestics in the labor force as well as for—it was hoped—their own future homes. The low pay, however regrettable, was accepted as a fact of life, and there were no efforts exerted to bring change in that area. After all, the women of the WCA themselves depended to a considerable degree upon low-paid domestics, a contradiction not readily grasped by the reformers.

The WCA was hopeful that a combination of strong religious faith and the ability to perform at least some type of honest work would ensure individual survival once a girl left the Refuge. They were taught sewing, and a laundry for profit was opened. In 1884 earnings from these endeavors reached somewhat over six hundred dollars, but collective efforts in money-making areas were never sufficient to meet the expenses of the home.[48] The WCA's emphasis was upon the necessity of performing "honorable" work despite low financial reward. If the girls could be steered away from their apparent tendencies toward opprobrium, then much was believed to have been accomplished.

It is difficult to determine how much success the Refuge achieved. The annual report for the Mission Home for 1883 noted that twenty-seven adults and thirty children had left that year; they went to live with friends or to homes and jobs that the WCA found for them. The report also stated that eight of those leaving for the year had done so without approval, two of whom had since returned. Inadequate information makes it impossible to speculate with certainty on the subsequent lives of Refuge residents. But the facts that the WCA continued this work well into the twentieth century in spite of difficulties with finances and public opinion and a few scattered letters from former residents attesting to the positive effects that the Refuge had on their lives[49] indicate that the WCA certainly believed they were achieving a measure of success — at least in respect to moral reformation. Another side of the coin may well have been that the reformers, vitally connected to a group in the process of status building, viewed sexually unorthodox behavior as a serious threat to the proper middle-class culture under construction. They had fashioned a definition of themselves within this society as moral redeemers, and in the process of redeeming the "fallen" had carved out new fields of activity for themselves which they would, therefore, have held onto with great tenacity. In any event, in the face of tough obstacles, work at the Refuge continued.

The Refuge remained a stepchild of the WCA and never became a very popular type of work among Memphis women in reform circles.[50] Still in the throes of overcoming their reluctance to act in public, work among prostitutes was an additional stigma. Supporters of the Refuge struggled constantly to win backers and influence public opinion. Apparently Memphis was not the only place where work of this type was greeted somewhat unenthusiastically. In an address to the International Conference of WCAs in St. Louis in 1881, Elizabeth Johnson spoke on the subject of the so-called fallen women. She urged compassion for them and called on all the associations to face the issue squarely and make that type of reformatory work a central concern. Mrs. Johnson pointed out that "the subject has only been introduced once before in our meetings and is considered a side issue." She accused churches of dying of self-righteousness and said, "Don't forget the Son of Man came to seek and save that which was lost."[51]

Johnson's own commitment was unwavering, and she and her husband personally bore most of the expense of the Mission Home

The Ella Oliver Refuge. The moral and social regeneration of "erring women" had been an objective of the Women's Christian Association since 1876. A home for these women went through several name changes and locations. In 1909, J. N. Oliver, in honor of his wife, donated funds for a new building, the Ella Oliver Refuge, on Walker Avenue. Reproduced from *Woman's Work in Tennessee* (Memphis: Printed under the auspices of the Tennessee Federation of Women's Clubs by Jones-Briggs Co., 1916).

for quite some time.[52] Even after his wife's death, J. C. Johnson continued to give financial support and donated some property for a possible future building site.[53]

It was also individual generosity that allowed expansion of the Refuge in 1909. Mrs. Jesse Brown, about whom it was said, "the one ambition of her life was the founding of a home for these unfortunate women,"[54] won the backing of J. N. Oliver, who donated the funds for a new building in honor of his wife. The new building, named the Ella Oliver Refuge, could accommodate seventy-five women and was equipped with its own chapel, infirmary, operating room, industrial room, modern kitchen, and separate matron's quarters.[55] While the Ella Oliver Refuge never received wide support from within the WCA, those who became involved were deeply committed, and the work done belied their numbers.

Among the Refuge advocates was Lide Meriwether, whose forceful position on society's responsibility for prostitutes was made public with the publication in 1872 of her book, *Soundings*. She did not mince words or fear to plunge into this taboo subject; she boldly accused society of gross hypocrisy and inconsistency in its cold-hearted victimization of young women. She unequivocally condemned the double standard, a constant theme in practically all ten sketches included in her book, and placed the blame for these lost souls squarely upon society's shoulders. She pointed an accusatory finger at "respectable" women who were themselves, Meriwether claimed, guilty of the "sin of omission" in not offering a hand to their sisters.[56] She charged that the erring man who had fallen into crime was always given another chance. "And mark well your husband's course toward his brethren . . . though he [an offender] should fall seventy and seven times, the same cordial and hearty hand is still offered to help him up again."[57] Such was not the practice for the fallen woman. Her sin is deemed "unpardonable," and she is shunned and condemned "into the very lowest strata of social life. . . . O consistency," said Meriwether, "thou art indeed a jewel!" She wondered out loud if for some reason men and women were subject to a different set of commandments.[58]

Meriwether was outraged by the gross injustice meted out to women, explaining that this was a major reason for the publication of her book. What she found especially horrifying and disappointing was the callous enforcement of the double standard upon women by other women. Throughout *Soundings* Meriwether urges "respectable" womanhood to rise up and join the ranks, admittedly small, in pioneering efforts to help these desperate ones, instead of condemning them.[59] There are "lost and dying wretches everywhere," said Meriwether; "is it not your bounden duty, and should you not deem it your God-given privilege, both to seek and to save?"[60] Consumed with the plight of women who were the "poorest of all 'God's poor,' in that they are the only class left utterly hopeless,"[61] Meriwether hoped that publication of these cases, of which she had personal knowledge, would awaken women to a new awareness of female responsibility for this social problem.

Soundings offered rare public condemnation of male sexual license in the South, a subject of deep psychological complexity. For a southern woman to make her views public on any subject in 1872 remained unusual, and Meriwether was fully aware of the consequences of "raising one's voice beyond the echo of our own hearthstone."[62] She warned others who might follow her lead to understand they were embarking upon a path "dark and narrow, steep and rugged."[63] She cautioned that the popular press would hold them up to "public scorn," and that "best friends will misjudge you. Those you have found kindhearted and liberal-handed in every other cause will fail you in this."[64] Nonetheless she urged, "Put your shoulder to the wheel,"[65] and make a reality of the boast "that we live in an age of civilization."[66]

That Meriwether intended to lambaste the double standard is eminently clear. To what extent her discourse was anti-male remains somewhat less clear. Her sketches are littered with deceitful males leading basically good, trusting girls astray, and she labels the typical husband of the good, church-going woman as "'in all human probability,' a reprobate and a heathen."[67] And yet, she points out, it was this very "heathen" male who displayed a much more humane attitude toward his fellow erring males than the "holy females" toward her erring sisters. Meriwether herself claimed her aim was not to condemn men: "My aim is to plead for women — I have no desire to anathematize man."[68] But her appeal to women to see this problem as theirs and to bear the responsibility for correcting it, implies the need to dictate and control male behavior to some degree. She condemns society's attitude toward unchaste women as wrongheaded and misconceived, with men and women both sharing culpability; but she puts the ball squarely in women's court to bring reform for the good of society generally and of women in particular.

Meriwether applauded the work of the Catholic priesthood and the Sisters of the Good Shepherd as being among the few "noble-hearted and charitable men and women of our day," who had addressed themselves to the problem of prostitution and had begun the work of establishing places of refuge for these "poor outcasts."[69] *Soundings* was dedicated to the Sisters of the Good Shepherd, who Meriwether felt had "truly offered themselves a living sacrifice upon the altar of womanhood."[70]

Lide Meriwether's *Soundings* offers a small glimpse into one Memphis woman's view of female sexuality which may contain wider

implications. While she disapproved of sex unsanctioned by marriage and supported efforts to help women avoid situations of temptation, she contended that, but for some twist of fate, any "respectable" woman could have found herself in the same situation as any
of the unfortunate girls depicted in *Soundings.* Implicit in Meriwether's writings is a recognition of sexuality in women as a common denominator, the only difference between "good" and "bad"
women being the context in which their sexuality was exercised.
This was quite a departure from the prescribed Victorian norm, expressed in the "cult of true womanhood," which posited that proper
ladies were largely sexless beings, "pure" women, whose lives were
confined to home and family.

While Memphis women were beginning to depart from their traditional sphere of activities, creating new identities outside of home
and family, there was also a new element of womanhood throughout urban America in the late nineteenth century—the single, independent, mobile young woman.[71] It was this new female ingredient whose sexuality was too often exercised in ways unsettling to
genteel society. Memphis women reformers, in addressing themselves to the "unchaste," and in attempting to enlist followers in
their work, found themselves face to face with a subject of great
complexity and subterranean meanings. While the prostitute was
a "nightmarish antithesis of the feminine ideal," violating all the
"beliefs and assumptions of civilized morality,"[72] the other side of
the coin was that the very life-style, attitudes, and behavior of such
women also pointed to signs of change in the feminine ideal.[73] To
deal with the issue of prostitution meant the necessity of dealing
with the whole issue of sexuality in all of its anxiety-provoking
complexity. Lide Meriwether had openly criticized genteel society,
exposing its mean and narrow outlines. She had addressed herself
to the issue of sexuality, recognizing its existence in women, and exposing the hypocrisy of society's differing response to men's and
women's exercise of it. While the WCA struggled to change the public perception of those labeled prostitutes, it usually did so on the
level of the need for Christian compassion and understanding. Memphis gentility, relatively new and insecure, fresh from throwing off
its frontier character, was attempting to construct, maintain, and

exhibit a proper middle-class culture. The WCA's religious impulse helped soften a harsh response to the effrontery of prostitution, but they were clearly not prepared to take a deep and critical look at the conventions of middle-class life, of which they themselves were major exponents. Prostitution was a subject whose lid, like Pandora's box, would best be kept shut.

The response of these Memphis women to prostitution stands in marked contrast to that of their northern sisters much earlier in the nineteenth century. The Boston Female Moral Reform Society had seethed: "Our mothers, our sisters, our daughters are sacrificed by the thousands every year on the alter of sin, and who are the agents in this work of destruction? Why, our fathers, our brothers, and our sons."[74] The Female Moral Reform Society of New York published the names of men suspected of immorality and succeeded in getting a bill passed making seduction a crime for the male participant.

Northern women had used a family allusion in expressing their outrage, accusing "fathers, brothers, and sons" as agents of destruction and betrayal, thus making men's actions especially reprehensible and exposure even more imperative. Southern women, on the other hand, would be much less likely to expose kin, even in generic terms, which may account for a more tentative response. In the more rural South, where the connective tissue among people was provided primarily by family, there had been few opportunities for women to develop support networks independent of their kinship group. Thus, while northern women in the 1830s had adequate homosocial support outside of family to enable them to challenge men's behavior openly and hold it up for public scorn and disapproval, Memphis women, indeed southern women generally, were just beginning to construct such links to each other in the late nineteenth century.

It seems a reasonable assumption that a number of the women of the WCA, having personal contact with outcast women and first-hand knowledge of their specific situations, would have harbored opinions much more critical of society's established attitudes than their public actions at the time revealed. But they were clearly not ready to be as publicly daring as northern women, or even as a Lide Meriwether on this particular subject, though many may have shared her views. Meriwether had once commented, "I am one of those creatures often heard of, but too seldom found—a happy woman,"[75] indicating a certain amount of frustration germinating beneath the surface.

The WCA generally viewed those who engaged in sexual activity unsanctioned by marriage as weak women who lacked sufficient strength to forgo temptation. There was little mention of their partners in such crime, and they did not, as a group, offer a critique of men's participation. The WCA solution to the problem of prostitution was to concentrate on the erring women themselves; and via an infusion of Christian faith, friendship, temporary shelter, and a new means of self-support, they believed redemption could come.

There were several other fertile fields of work that occupied the WCA, and elicited a somewhat broader-based and more enthusiastic response from within the organization. Among these was the project "everywhere recognized as the peculiar central and essential field of WCA endeavor," which was the establishment of a boarding home for "unprotected" working girls.[76] With the opening of the Young Women's Boarding Home in October 1887,[77] the WCA felt it was proceeding with work that was at the heart of what they were trying to accomplish in society: helping women help themselves. "Perhaps no call from the president of the WCA to philanthropic work met with such hearty and enthusiastic response by the women of our city as this."[78] The WCA viewed this particular project as their major concern, believing they had a responsibility "to guard the well being of working women, not only physically, morally, and socially but from the economic standpoint."[79] As the *Annual Directory of the W & YWCA* expressed it, their purpose was to "furnish a home for unprotected, self-supporting women where their physical, mental and spiritual welfare will be promoted."[80]

As the commercial center for a large surrounding rural area, Memphis was a natural magnet for migrants. The population grew significantly in the decades of the 1880s and 1890s.[81] Included were a number of unskilled young women who were "determined upon a course of independent self-support, as strangers, without means at their command, exposed to temptations and without protection."[82]

Whereas many viewed the Refuge "as a futile attempt to reclaim the irreclaimable,"[83] the Young Women's Boarding Home seemed a clear case of young women who were making honorable efforts to support themselves and were successfully resisting temptations to which other "weaker" women had fallen victim. As Clara Conway expressed it, these were not "pensioners on your bounty," but girls who "are working to help themselves."[84] Such young women seemed more deserving of a helping hand than candidates for the Refuge, and it was much easier for middle- and upper-class Memphians to identify with them. Here were "vast numbers" of young women, many "tenderly cared for in their early years" and often well educated, who "owing to misfortunes in life," had to care for themselves.[85] Their road was a hard one. As Clara Conway pointed out, society did not understand the working girl's hardship. She was on her feet most of the day for about five dollars per week and was often the breadwinner for her entire family, which remained in rural areas.[86] The WCA believed she needed the protective shield of family; if not an actual family, at least a reasonable facsimile, and this the Young Women's Boarding Home strove to provide. A boarding home could provide "wholesome companionship when their work is over," and homelike comforts such as reading matter, musical instruments, and prayer.[87] It was a place where additional skills could be learned, and plans were laid to develop training classes and lecture courses to educate young women to be independent.[88]

The boarding home also assisted girls in finding employment and provided a fund to help those temporarily out of work or whose wages were not yet sufficient for survival. As in a family, the Young Women's Boarding Home wanted to be supportive until the girl could "get on her feet." A small fee of twenty-five cents was paid to the boarding home to defray the expense of placing her in a job, and weekly board was charged based on a girl's wages although no one paid more than $3.25.[89] The WCA wanted to emphasize the necessity of "paying one's way" in the world and constantly reiterated the themes of self-help, independence, and self-sufficiency.

The WCA, via the boarding home, believed they were helping "solve the most difficult and significant industrial problem of the day," which was the "well-being of the working-woman. The industrial well-being of the whole country," they believed "is determined by the rate of wages and the standard of comfort the woman-worker is able to maintain."[90] They firmly believed they were doing their part by providing a lodging place with a "home atmosphere" which was "comfortable and beneficial in both temporal and spiritual respects so that young strangers will find it a privilege to become one of the family."[91]

The rhetoric of the WCA clearly reveals their belief in the family as the anchor in a cold business world. It was "unfortunate" for women to have to leave the safe world of domesticity, but since necessity demanded it they could at least find comfort and stability in an ersatz home such as the Young Women's Boarding Home. In this way, the reforming women felt they were performing an important service by injecting the stabilizing influences of family into an increasingly commercial world. They left their own homes in order to spread their maternal and sisterly influence, and they were increasingly encouraged and congratulated for doing so.[92]

The Young Women's Boarding Home enjoyed great success. Individuals, both men and women, and various organizations and churches helped finance the project. Rented quarters sufficed until 1890 when the WCA bought a house on Shelby Street with accommodations for fifty-five boarders and room for expansion.[93] The financial decision to purchase this sixteen-thousand-dollar structure was made jointly by a committee of the association's board of directors and an advisory committee of men.[94]

A very active and aggressive building drive was launched by the WCA and carried on for several years. Contributions were solicited, the city's newspapers provided impetus via publicity, and a variety of fund raisers were held by members of the WCA.[95] The response from the community was very positive, but the depression in 1892 slowed their efforts. Not to be stopped at this point, two WCA members, Miss Ella Guy and Mrs. Mary Wormeley, convinced Hugh L. Brinkley, a wealthy Memphis landowner, to pay the remaining indebtedness of six thousand dollars as a memorial to his mother, Anne Brinkley.[96] In return, the Young Women's Boarding Home became the Anne Brinkley Home. Upon his death in 1905, Brinkley left an additional forty thousand dollars, which provided a new seven-story building at Second and Pontotoc Streets and allowed the association ample space for classes to educate young women for industrial jobs and in such domestic arts as cooking and sewing.[97] The Anne Brinkley Home became the headquarters for the whole WCA, and in 1926 a two-story annex was added making it possible to accommodate as many as two hundred girls.[98]

The Anne Brinkley Home was as close as Memphis came to having something that approximated the settlement-house idea. Wage-earning women there found a haven and received support and access to various types of training. It also provided a place for the city's elite, educated women, who searched for stimulation beyond their homes and sought outlets for their need to participate in the excitement of the growth and development of the city. In such work as that of the Anne Brinkley Home, they could derive a sense of achievement in the belief that they were applying themselves to solutions to pressing social problems. Here rich and poor interacted, contributing to the incubation period of a female support network in Memphis. Clara Conway, in addressing the fifteenth anniversary meeting of the WCA in 1890, said she believed WCA work had made the rich more aware of "real suffering," creating empathy and "a strong bond of sympathy between rich and poor."[99]

The women of the WCA, through the Anne Brinkley Home, hardly revolutionized women's place in the commercial world of Memphis. They did, however, succeed in focusing attention upon a developing social problem and took some tentative steps toward addressing it. Their fund-raising success clearly attests to significant community support for their endeavors. But, as was the case in attempts to deal with prostitution in Memphis via the Refuge, their range of vision was very narrow. The WCA genuinely believed that the young women with whom they were concerned could, through diligent application of skills, become self-reliant individuals in a capitalist society. Thus the WCA concentrated on preparing young women to enter the marketplace, but largely on the terms dictated by the marketplace. They spoke of "kind-hearted merchants who applied to the Young Women's Boarding Home for help,"[100] without commenting on the fact of long hours, low pay, and exceedingly slim hopes for advancement. They were sincerely

The Anne Brinkley Home. The Women's Christian Association originally established a Young Women's Boarding Home in 1887. It was renamed the Anne Brinkley Home in 1892 in memory of the mother of Hugh L. Brinkley, a generous supporter. The above building was made possible by an additional bequest by Brinkley in 1905. This seven-story building served as a boarding home for young working women and also became the headquarters for the whole WCA. Reproduced from *Woman's Work in Tennessee* (Memphis: Printed under the auspices of the Tennessee Federation of Women's Clubs by Jones-Briggs Co., 1916.)

desirous of creating a more caring human community in Memphis; but ultimately an uncritical acceptance of the ideology of liberal capitalism, with its concomitants of competitive, possessive individualism and a male-dominated hierarchy, prevented meaningful reform.[101] The women possessed an uncompromising belief in an individual's ability to better one's material circumstances by the application of personal effort. Charity, perhaps necessary in certain desperate situations, was basically something to be avoided as it was viewed as damaging to ambition. They reasoned further that charity would keep wage-earning women from seeking better pay, thus compromising their industrial independence. Charity was artificial, a potential detriment to the free flow of society and the virtues of independence and self-help. The WCA took great care to point out that they were not asking for charity for the Anne Brinkley Home, but for an endowment.[102] Once paid for, the home would be independent and self-supporting, and the public would not be asked for further financial support. They were requesting a boost, that was all. The WCA stressed that the boarding home should not be considered in the same light as the Children's Home and the Refuge, "which are completely eleemosynary institutions. To allow this is to surely defeat these brave breadwinning girls."[103]

While these reformers felt genuine compassion for women who faced many obstacles in finding a place in the commercial world, the machinery necessary to form a particularly female perspective on the urban, industrial condition was lacking. The middle class tended to view the need of women to work for wages as unfortunate, a temporary condition, it was hoped, to be relieved by marriage. There were some professional women among the WCA membership, and Elizabeth Lyle Saxon had commented on the presence of female architects and engineers in Memphis, saying optimistically: "What a stride in twenty years. . . . No need now to marry for a home . . . no longer a drone in the home and the world, no longer a gossip but a well-educated, trained, human being."[104] Saxon's comment, made in about the mid-1880s, represented premature enthusiasm for the development of any significant number of economically independent and autonomous women in Memphis. While working women were increasingly afforded respectability, wage work was not a condition to which very many women aspired. The influence of middle-class identity and the economic realities of life in the late nineteenth century, which usually meant female dependence on a male breadwinner, remained predominant. A main objective of the WCA was to help women through difficult situations which were viewed largely as temporary. Few, although there were some, promoted the development of professionalism for women. It would also take longer experience in the developing commercial, urban setting to see that wage-earning women's lives belied the truth of such middle-class tenets as hard work and diligent application of skills automatically begetting success and self-sufficiency.

By their fifteenth anniversary in 1890, the number of dues-paying members of the WCA had reached 450, with about one-quarter of that number being actively engaged in the association's projects.[105] Those whose contribution was solely financial were associate members, and auxiliary members were men who assisted the women in various ways.[106] In addition to the Refuge, the Children's Home, and the Anne Brinkley Home, the WCA work included a woman's exchange, which provided a market for articles made by women trying to support themselves and their families, and a wide variety of missionary efforts in hospitals, jails, and asylums.

In November 1881, the WCA began publication of their own journal, *The Gleaner*, which was an excellent vehicle for disseminating information about women's work both locally and nationally as well as providing further opportunity for local talent. The women edited, published, and managed *The Gleaner* entirely by themselves and had good local patronage as well as "considerable circulation" scattered throughout the country.[107] *The Gleaner's* financial history was described as "unique," in that it began with virtually no capital and soon was entirely self-supporting and free of debt. Their journal gained quite a respected reputation and was said to be "another recognition of the power of the press in fostering any enterprise, [seeking] especially to build up and strengthen the unity, intelligence and usefulness of Christian women."[108]

The WCA represented a large step by elite women of Memphis into the public world. They had emerged as a unified body of socially concerned women possessed of great creative vitality, whose beneficial impact upon the city was increasingly recognized. They were the essential ingredient in a number of reform projects, and by the mid-1880s their public presence was an accomplished and accepted fact.

Engaged as they were in aiding citizens in desperate situations, for which municipal provisions were either nonexistent or sadly inadequate, collaboration between the WCA and municipal authorities developed. The city often referred people to WCA institutions;[109] and, in 1890, Chief of Police Davis recommended the establishment of a home for wayward boys along the lines of work being done by the WCA on behalf of girls.[110] The women exphasized government's responsibility to provide them with financial backing, and the Tennessee legislature passed a bill providing that certain fines collected by the Taxing District should be set aside for the benefit of reformatory work. However, in 1881 the WCA complained that no money had ever been received. The women also petitioned the county court in 1884 to provide funds to enable them to take over the care and education of young girls whom the WCA considered inappropriately placed in the poor house.[111] While the response from government was invariably insufficient, the validity of the women's argument for greater public responsibility had been forcefully presented and would at length be recognized.

The WCA also enlisted support from private male citizens, who as auxiliary members accompanied the women in their ward visiting and in other areas where "the presence and leadership of various Christian gentlemen"[112] was deemed helpful. Men usually presided over the WCA annual meetings, presenting the reports that had been prepared by women. In 1889, the WCA's house-to-house visitation work was merged into the male-led Christmas Club,[113] which itself was incorporated into the United Charities in 1893. Some have suggested that male involvement and assumption of leadership roles in philanthropic work previously dominated by women signified an assault upon female autonomy, others that it was a male capitulation to female values.[114] In the case of the WCA in Memphis, the women were naive in the ways of institutional control and accepted male participation without comment. To those women in the habit of thinking in terms of male predominance, collaboration may well have translated into legitimation of their own actions and been interpreted as success in widening their base of support. It seemed perfectly natural to the women that the WCA's house-to-house visitation project should be subsumed into the Christmas Club, thus avoiding duplication of activities. No doubt in 1900 it also seemed efficient and practical that the WCA Children's Home be absorbed into the Leath Orphan's Home, where ultimate authority rested with a board of seven male trustees. Calling upon occasional male participation and allowing some WCA activities to be split away and incorporated into groups where men exercised ultimate direction or control posed no conscious threat to the Memphis women. They saw such developments in terms of what seemed best for the recipients of the charity and not from the standpoint of organizational control.

Women's participation in WCA work had brought them together in numerous communal projects. Their shared experiences and co-operation had increased their collective sense of sisterhood as well as their individual feelings of self-esteem and self-confidence. Female networks aside from family were beginning to crystallize, and a distinct and discernible movement of women making a public testament took shape. Increment by increment Memphis women inched their way toward a new definition of their role in society.

3

The Woman's Christian
Temperance Union

The Women's Christian Association represented an important step in feminine assertiveness and provided women with new channels for their ambitions. Their activities seemed to engender more activities. While the WCA was composed of church-connected women, in the latter 1880s and into the 1890s there followed a whole host of female associational efforts deriving their inspiration from a variety of sources. As female competence and ability crept into the prescriptive sketch of elite womanhood, their involvement in reform efforts was increasingly accepted and options for women via voluntary associations increased impressively.

The outlook of the city in general during the latter decades of the nineteenth century was decidedly optimistic. The worst appeared behind them, as the devastating yellow-fever epidemic of 1878 had passed, and by the early 1890s citizens believed the Taxing District government was well along in untangling the knotty problems that had hampered "the bluff city" to the point of calling its continued existence into question. D. P. Hadden, president of the Taxing District, articulated the sentiment of many when he commented in 1889 that he knew of no city that could claim a brighter future.[1] He was referring to revived financial stability and returning prosperity among the business class. But as the population doubled in the decade of the 1880s and continued to increase in the 1890s, strains on city services were again evident. Quality of life had been and increasingly would be the concern of white, elite women, whose developing sense of public responsibility propelled them into a new role of influencing the direction of municipal recovery.

In pursuit of their desire for "usefulness" outside the "home circle," the women found that the Woman's Christian Temperance Union served them well. An outgrowth of temperance crusades in Ohio and New York in 1873 and temperance activities related to the National Sunday School Assembly at Chautauqua, New York, in 1874, the WCTU was organized in November 1874, at a meeting in Cleveland, Ohio. A national women's temperance society was formed by "welding into a national force the necessary number of temperance leagues that had begun to function independently under the Crusade impetus."[2] Belle Kearney, a leading advocate of temperance in Mississippi, described the WCTU as "the golden key that unlocked the prison doors of pent-up possibilities. It was the generous liberator, the joyous iconoclast, the discoverer, the developer of Southern women."[3]

The WCTU was led by Annie Wittenmyer for the first four years of its existence. Under her direction, gospel temperance and moral suasion were the initial means used in working towards the goal of abstinence. The women worked to secure pledges of total abstinence by convincing people of the evils of drink. Ultimately they came to rely more on political means, and their aims shifted to legally closing neighborhood saloons and prohibiting all liquor sales.[4] Their campaign was directed at men, as serious drinking in the nineteenth century was considered a male prerogative and men were perceived as the chief users and abusers of alcohol. Liquor, and male misuse of it, were viewed as major threats to family stability and the home, and drinking came to be associated with wife beating, neglect, and desertion. "Break down the American home and the fabric of free government goes down with it," reasoned the temperance women[5] as they reanointed the home and family as society's anchor.

In Memphis, Elizabeth Johnson, the workhorse of the Women's Christian Association, played the key role in organizing women for active involvement in temperance work. She had been present at the national organizing convention of the WCTU, and was appointed a vice-president for Tennessee.[6] Two years later, Annie Wittenmyer, accompanied by the vice-president of the New Jersey union, a Mrs. Denham, came to Memphis to help generate support for a local chapter. A large crowd at the Court Street Cumberland Presbyterian Church heard Wittenmyer speak on temperance, her remarks being described as "lengthy, but interesting and instructive."[7] Shortly thereafter, in March 1876, a local chapter was founded.[8]

Women of varied description were urged to become involved in the temperance cause—young, old, married, or single. Even if they would not be active, they were urged to join—if only to lend the weight of their names and presence. "Women can do much by joining and pledging not to use alcohol in their homes and not to associate with young men who do."[9] They were urged to teach by example, which was considered the strongest of all arguments.

In 1878 Johnson presented a written progress report at the WCTU annual convention in Baltimore. Memphis women had persuaded six thousand people to pledge abstinence, including many of the city's most prominent men. Weekly meetings were being held in the Congregational Church, and work was beginning to be extended into Mississippi, Arkansas, and northern Alabama.[10] Even amid such promising progress, Johnson mentioned the dual obstacles of apathy on the part of many women and outright resistance from some Memphis churchmen. She commented that while she felt a "grand awakening" was beginning to occur among women, there could be a much "grander one when you can convince them that Paul does not excuse them much less forbid them speaking out their minds on this temperance question."[11] Apathy and reluctance among Memphis women to inject themselves into public issues remained a barrier to organization. The reappearance of yellow fever in 1879 also appears to have been a factor retarding the Memphis movement, so that by the end of that year the national organization was lamenting the lack of progress in the South—although Johnson was mentioned as one who was putting forth great efforts. The "Committee on Southern Work" cited "timidity on the part of southern women" as a hindrance and urged more leadership from the national WCTU.[12]

The movement in Memphis was reenergized with the arrival of Frances Willard in 1881. The magnetic Willard had succeeded Wittenmyer as president of the national WCTU in 1879. Under Willard's leadership the objectives of the WCTU were greatly expanded

to encompass a long list of social issues, although temperance remained the cement holding everything together.[13] As Frances Willard's
"do everything" philosophy was explained by a WCTU member: "We
are trying to type for the world a new kind of Womanhood, with
brains large enough to understand the misery of the world, and
with a heart as large as the brain, that can feel not only in our own
dear circle of home, but for all humanity, and calls nothing human
foreign to ourselves."[14]

The rebirth of WCTU activity in 1881 has sometimes been mis-
taken for the initial appearance of that organization in Memphis.
Indeed, the work was taken up that year with considerable enthusiasm, and a state organization was formed shortly thereafter. While
the WCTU was more successful in attracting Tennessee women to
the cause in the 1880s, growth remained uneven, and recruiting in
the South was not without its difficulties. Mary T. Lathrap of the
national WCTU likened working in the South to "drilling rock."[15]

Willard herself harbored doubts about her reception in that part
of the country. She would be delivering a public message, and was
a northern woman in addition to being a temperance woman. But
Willard made a very favorable impression on southern women,
and her personal appearances were important in winning support.
Her success was due in part to her own dynamism as well as the
strong backing she received from respected southern women in the
communities she visited—Elizabeth Johnson in Memphis being an
excellent example.

Southerners were impressed by Willard's speaking ability, and,
equally important, they perceived her as a very "womanly woman."
She was described glowingly as being "so sisterly and so motherly,
with a divine mind."[16] Caroline Merrick of New Orleans, said Willard did more than any other person in the nineteenth century to
"widen the outlook and develop the mental aspirations of women."[17]

Willard was very careful in the South to stress the theme of women
waging war for "God and Home and Native Land." As was the case
with the WCA in Memphis, women were being offered an opportunity to assert themselves on behalf of a very lofty and eminently
respectable cause. The WCTU provided another noncontroversial
outlet for women to develop their capabilities, expand female net-

works, and exercise authority in the public sphere. The initial re-sistance of churchmen to this more public role for women was gradually transformed into support. Though unable to quarrel with the women's defense of the home, the ministers continued to be somewhat uneasy with women who were no longer content to con-fine their activities to church "janitress" and who seemed to be "searching for the preacher within themselves."[18]

At the WCTU annual meeting in 1882, which was held in Louis-ville, Kentucky, the Reverend J. C. Morris addressed himself to Saint Paul's strictures regarding women. Elizabeth Johnson and a group from Memphis were in attendance. Morris testified that as a young man, based on Paul's teaching, he had harbored the "bitterest preju-dice" against women's work in public. Now he urged that Paul's words be interpreted in the light of the social customs of that remote era and not as a statement of any sort of divine authority. Morris said he believed the time had come for women to be freed from silence, and he urged them on in their work.[19] At the fourteenth annual meeting, held in Nashville in 1887, the WCTU happily acknowl-edged endorsement from three Methodist conferences, three Presby-terian synods, and a number of Baptist associations.[20]

In Memphis, there were an estimated ninety-five WCTU mem-bers by 1882, and *The Gleaner* commented that the "Great ground-swell in favor of prohibition is slowly but surely pervading the think-ing classes everywhere."[21] WCTU branches had been formed in both leading girls' schools, Miss Conway's and Miss Higbee's; and toward the end of 1882 the WCTU provided the impetus for the establishment of an industrial school for girls, with evening classes being held in the rooms of the Hope Night School.[22]

Several Memphis women involved in the WCA had also become active in temperance work, tightening the developing network among local women and providing a base of support from which further-reaching efforts could be launched. Ellen Watson, for example, would succeed Elizabeth Johnson as president of the WCA upon the lat-ter's death in 1883. Both had been charter members of the WCA and subsequently worked together in temperance activities. Virtu-ally all the officers of the Memphis WCTU in 1895 were conspic-uous in the WCA.[23] When the Tennessee WCTU was organized in

October 1882, Memphis women occupied prominent leadership roles. Elizabeth Johnson became that group's first president, Mrs. Douglas Walworth was elected corresponding secretary, and Ellen Watson was treasurer. Thus, these Memphis women were exercising leadership outside their immediate community as they worked to create a state organization to facilitate temperance activities throughout Tennessee. The state organization also bought them into contact with women from all over Tennessee who shared similar interests and goals, providing another channel through which a sense of sisterhood could develop.

Only six months after becoming state president, Elizabeth Johnson died, a devastating loss to the women and the movement. Soon after, however, the Tennessee union engaged the indefatigable Elizabeth Lyle Saxon to become state organizer. Saxon, working closely with Lide Meriwether, who became president of the Tennessee WCTU in 1884, brought a new vigor and forcefulness to temperance in Tennessee.[24]

Writer, lecturer, temperance and suffrage worker, Elizabeth Lyle Saxon spent her adulthood working "to help heal the hurts of the daughters of my people."[25] Saxon's energetic dedication took her throughout the South and Southwest and included a few sojourns in the East as well. She became very prominent in Memphis reform circles and provided an important link to national figures.

Saxon, a native Tennessean, was born in Greeneville in 1832 but was reared in Alabama and spent several years in New York City after her marriage to a South Carolinian with northern business interests. She first came to Memphis during the Civil War in search of her father, who had been imprisoned in Irving Block as a confederate spy. He died shortly after Saxon arranged his release. After the war, she rejoined her husband in New Orleans, where business had taken him. Saxon subsequently divided her time between New Orleans and Memphis and became immersed in reform work in both cities.[26]

Saxon's father, Andrew Lyle, had enormous influence upon his daughter's life. Her mother died when Saxon was two years old, leaving responsibility for the child in the hands of the father. Andrew Lyle became his daughter's idol, and Saxon described herself as being very much like him: "I was the child of his soul as well as his body."[27] He bequeathed to her his love of literature and nature and his hatred of oppression.[28] Lyle, who was described as a man of "liberal culture" with a "broad view of life,"[29] had very advanced ideas concerning the development and sphere of women. He sent his daughter to be formally educated in the school of a noted southern author, Caroline Lee Hentz, in Tuskeegee, Alabama. An aspiring writer, at the age of twelve Saxon began publishing short stories and sketches in various southern newspapers.[30]

She married Lydale Saxon of Lorraine District, South Carolina, in 1848. They ultimately had seven children, four of whom survived into adulthood. Living in New York at the time the Civil War began, Elizabeth Saxon described the day Alabama seceded as one of the saddest in her life. She and her husband were unionists, but when war came she returned to Alabama, describing herself as "Southern in every vein and fibre of being."[31] While she had "gloried in the unflinching courage shown by Wendell Phillips and Henry Ward Beecher" on the slavery issue, feeling women labored under similar injustices, Saxon nevertheless believed her first loyalty lay with the South. Despite that loyalty, as a person of unionist sentiment who harbored doubts about a slave system, the two years she lived in Alabama just after the outbreak of war were extremely difficult ones. She later said:

> For quite a while men gave free voice to their disaffection and sympathy with the Union, but overwhelmed by the voice of numbers wild with excitement, declaring it dangerous in the midst of existing conditions to voice such sentiments, one after another became silent, awed at the bitterness and hostility shown such sentiments. And let every man and woman remember this: We lived, as it were, over a powder magazine, that a careless word might arouse as a spark would powder; and it meant ruin to many. . . . It was actions growing out of this condition of things that made my life a living fever of dread during the two weary years I remained in Alabama. Brought up in the little town, I loved all its inhabitants as if they were literally "my very own people," and I knew the underlying Union sentiment of many a silent-voiced man, compelled to go to war or furnish a substitute. . . . If hell can furnish a more horrible condition than fell to such people and their female friends, I don't believe it.[32]

Saxon's husband, not prepared to face possible financial ruin and loss of life on behalf of the southern cause, hired a substitute. When that alternative was no longer possible, he returned to New York where he remained until the war ended. Saxon herself became a "Southern Mother" in Memphis, and worked day and night for suffering soldiers. She later described the incessant activity of women who, she said, worked "so far into the night that tears dimmed their eyes until they could hardly see." She described the toll of starvation on "thousands of children" and the desperate lack of medicine. She recalled writing obituaries and being glad, when printing was suspended because of a shortage of paper, that she did not have to write them anymore. Said Saxon: "My pen fails to portray our misery. . . . I would wonder in blind pain where is there a God, and does He rule in the affairs of men?"[33]

Saxon's intellect and perception made her feel very keenly the sting of subordination common to nineteenth-century women. She viewed women as an oppressed class and equated their position in society with that of slavery, saying "I saw that it teemed with injustice and shame to all womankind, and I hated it." She felt deeply what she considered the shame of women's repression, and said, "I really think the hardest and meanest things I ever had to hear were spoken on this question."[34]

For Saxon, the key to women's future lay with voting rights and economic opportunity, placing her squarely in the advance guard of the women's rights movement. She believed suffrage would allow women to unlock all the other doors of opportunity, and to the pioneers in this work she offered paeans of praise: "It was this staunch band of pioneers, defying criticism, scorn and hate, who forced open college doors, invaded the law courts and stubbornly contested every inch of ground so persistently held by fraud or force from the daughters of the great republic."[35]

In the 1870s Saxon became one of New Orleans's leading exponents of woman suffrage. In conjunction with a group of kindred women, Saxon secured a petition for equal suffrage signed by over six hundred of New Orleans's prominent citizens. In June 1879, she addressed the Louisiana Constitutional Convention on that subject, asking for justice, not charity, and was well received. Mrs.

Caroline Merrick, wife of the Chief Justice of Louisiana, and Saxon's close partner in reform, also spoke. At first Merrick hesitated at speaking before the legislature, fearing she would not be heard, and suggested her son-in-law might read her words. But Saxon told her: "No matter if they do not hear a word you say! You do not wish a man to represent you at the polls; represent yourself, now, if you only stand up and move your lips."[36]

While the Louisiana women succeeded in getting only a crumb — women were made eligible for school offices — it was, Saxon believed, a "prophetic crumb" of a "surely preparing loaf."[37]

Following her suffrage work in New Orleans, Saxon's public career began to flourish. She went to Washington, D. C., with Susan B. Anthony and addressed a suffrage convention, as well as making a speaking appearance before the Senate Judiciary Committee. She and Anthony toured New England on behalf of woman suffrage, and subsequently Saxon found herself in great demand all over the country. She was considered an "impassioned orator" whose speeches elicited enthusiastic responses: They were "stirring," "the whole state is ringing with her praise," "the call for an encore was unanimous," and she "had fairly electrified the state."[38]

After her suffrage tour with Anthony, Saxon canvassed six counties in New York state for the National Prohibition Alliance, and in 1882 she also began organizaing chapters for the WCTU.[39] Thus, when Saxon became state organizer for the WCTU in Tennessee in 1884, she was already a seasoned campaigner, merging temperance and social purity with suffrage as dual goals. While most southerners remained wary of woman suffrage, seeing it as the "left wing" of the nineteenth-century woman question, Saxon nudged them along. If the "great problem of human liberty" was ever to be solved and "sex slavery" ended, women's rights, she believed, had to be expanded.[40] She felt she was working in the cause of human freedom, and to be a pioneer in such work was to engage in a noble effort — hardly something overly bold or shameless, as it was sometimes described. Her father had impressed upon her the "deep and terrible meaning" of the parable of the talents and believed no man or woman had any right to withhold themselves from any work for which they were fitted. To Elizabeth Saxon freedom meant

God's law on earth. Andrew Lyle had taught his daughter that to work for reforms for women was the highest duty and on his deathbed had asked her to promise "never to cease working for unfortunate women so long as her life should last."[41] She was willing to endure "unpleasant remarks, uncounted opprobrium and pecuniary loss" in order to keep her pledge "never to fail in the work he had taught me was my highest duty."[42] Very likely another factor in such certitude and her ability to press on in the face of criticism was Saxon's belief that she possessed a "sixth sense," which gave her special insight into life's mysteries. She believed that in time science would discover that there were other senses in human beings not yet developed:

> My own impression founded on my own experience, is that all spirituality is as far as possible killed in children by their parents. We admit man is possessed of five senses, and if anything savoring of a higher, or more subtle sense is shown, instantly it is deemed uncanny unnatural, and must be repressed.[43]

Saxon felt it especially important for women to recognize such possibilities, as "woman in her weakness is ever to be made the victim unless she strives for individuality, and learns the difficult lesson 'know thyself.'"[44]

Saxon's father had been supportive and sympathetic towards her belief in her sixth sense. "He alone seemed . . . to understand my nature and to sympathize with my startling statements. He had found that I did see and knew of events that occurred miles away, as was more than once verified by him."[45] Throughout her life she had visions and prophetic dreams, one of which involved the specific circumstances of her father's death. The fulfillment of this dream, Saxon said, "made me a firm believer in special providence, or of some influence that the world at large little understood and generally scoffs at."[46]

Saxon had the courage of her convictions and never wavered in her reform efforts. Her sixth sense may have accustomed her to the scoffing of critics, and she was not discouraged by disapproval or skepticism. All her statements reveal a self-assured individual, convinced of the rightness of her actions. Saxon described herself as being "like the ancient hero," who when menaced with death for warning his people of their danger cried "Strike me dead, but hear me first."[47] Very much in the risk-taking tradition charted by Elizabeth and Lide Meriwether, Saxon provided a role model for Memphis women and other southerners whose temperaments were more conditioned to remaining out of the public eye.

While thought to be well in advance of her time, Saxon was not regarded as overly strident, and she exercised great influence over men and women alike. The *Memphis Daily Appeal* described her as a woman of "genius and thought," who was a "recognized power" in politics and numbered some of the nation's "greatest and most learned men" among her personal friends.[48] She was regarded as a respectable "Southern Lady," and was very secure in Memphis social circles.[49]

In her reform efforts Saxon was often joined by Lide Meriwether, who likewise believed that via the WCTU and similar organizations, the woman of the nineteenth century would "find herself" and would take her "rightful place in the world."[50] Meriwether was in perfect harmony with Saxon's belief that in women lay the future of civilization, saying, "All the charitable work that is done in this country is done by women. The men do not do a single thing, and the only moral hope of the country lies in the women."[51]

When Lide Meriwether became president of the Tennessee WCTU in 1884, she confessed to feeling thrust into a somewhat unfamiliar role: "This was only the second time I had ever been within sight or sound of an organized convention of any kind, conducted by either men or women."[52] The work both fascinated and suited her, and she was enormously successful. She and Saxon, whose responsibility as state organizer entailed the formation and instruction of new unions, constituted a dynamic partnership. When they assumed their leadership roles there had been seven unions in Tennessee. The two women undertook an extensive traveling schedule, speaking and organizing; and by 1887 Tennessee could boast 210 unions with a membership of about 2,500.[53] Elizabeth Saxon felt she "had been consecrated anew to the glorious work of humanity" and commented, "I felt women were indeed arousing to the fact that they did hold some power."[54]

The progress in Tennessee was part of an expanding interest in temperance throughout the South. Because the national WCTU viewed the region as a difficult one in which to make inroads, it was designated a "department" of the WCTU, much like a foreign mission area. For a time it was headed by Mrs. Sallie Chapin of Charleston, South Carolina. Once again, dynamic leadership proved to be critical. Chapin, credited with being the most important single force in the WCTU's success in the South,[55] was an indefatigable organizer and energizer who traveled extensively, proselytizing among her southern sisters. She was full of praise for Lide Meriwether and Elizabeth Saxon, whose backgrounds were, not surprisingly, very similar to her own.[56]

The WCTU offered southern women a respectable forum from which they could both perform their duty as defenders of the nineteenth-century home and family and simultaneously exercise their growing desire to widen that very "sphere" to which they had been assigned. Defending the home and family now seemed to require public action, which many women found extremely exciting and promising. Their impact upon society could be more direct, and they reached out eagerly to the new roles that presented themselves. Sallie Chapin, for example, was convinced that the WCTU was the key to a spiritually reunified United States, and in her welcoming address at the WCTU convention in 1881 in Washington, she said:

> No North, no South, no alien name,
> Firm in the cause we stand;
> Hearts melted in the sacred flame
> For God and native land.[57]

Indeed, as Ruth Bordin has pointed out, bringing northern and southern women together in a voluntary organization was, in itself, an enormous accomplishment.[58] There were many sources of anxiety between them, and—just as Frances Willard had experienced doubt as to her reception in the South—Chapin was reluctant about going north. But her encounter with northern temperance women allayed her fears.

> I have been North this summer; I have attended a great many of these temperance meetings, and your love has been to my darkened life what I

did not suppose could ever come there again, and I wanted my Southern sisters to come and know you as I know you, and then I knew they would love you as I do with all my heart.[59]

As increased contact between northern and southern women occurred, such feelings as those expressed by Chapin spread. The women not only gained confidence from each other, but also felt they were making an important contribution toward furthering national unity. The Mississippi state union in 1886 reported to the national WCTU that they welcomed northern speakers and that they viewed reform efforts as "the final breaking down of sectional prejudice. We want to stand face to face with you in the North, heart answering heart, and hand in hand. Thus united, to work for our common cause."[60]

Lide Meriwether, in welcoming women from all over the country to a national WCTU convention in Nashville in 1887, said:

Do not imagine that because you have set your feet upon Southern soil you are to bind up heart and soul and brain in the old cast-off clothes of conservatism. On Tennessee soil you are to think, and speak, and act precisely as seemeth good in your own sight. Our state needs a good shaking up — don't be afraid to give it. The conservative diet upon which we have subsisted has produced a good deal of moral, mental, and political dyspepsia, and a little unusual exercise in the tumbling about of old ideas would be very wholesome. . . . We White Ribboners have learned to trust, and to love our comrades from every section.[61]

Along with the healing of sectional antagonism, race was another delicate issue addressed by the WCTU. While integration was rare even in the North, there was cooperation between black and white women on the temperance issue. Black women were organized into unions, with the impetus coming from the white women. The white attitude was indeed somewhat patronizing: Sallie Chapin said at the WCTU annual meeting in 1881 that liquor was again making slaves of black men. "Under slavery they were a responsibility greater than children but who is responsible for them now? The nation should take care of them."[62] Prohibition was, she believed, the answer and the nation's duty. Yet despite such a bias, temperance did provide a basis for contact and the possibility of mutual under-standing among black and white women.

Spearheaded by Lide Meriwether, the first efforts to organize southern black women on behalf of temperance resulted in a meet-ing in Memphis in 1886. Meriwether presided over the interracial group, probably a "first" in Memphis, and in her address gave all possible encouragement. She said she would rejoice in this new "war for freedom."[63] Out of this convention a black WCTU group was established and officers elected, the president being Mrs. C. H. Phillips of Memphis, wife of the pastor of Collins Chapel, who was himself a strong proponent of temperance. All four officers of the new union had been classmates at Fisk University in Nashville. Two of the four had married ministers, and another a state legis-lator who was described as "a power among his people."[64]

Wives, mothers, well educated, these young black women — most of whom were also teachers — were anxious to participate in work they deemed essential to the future progess of their race. As women, they found common ground with their white counterparts. In the following year, 1887, two black women representing fourteen black unions in Tennessee attended the state WCTU convention, present-ing reports that were highly commended. Tennessee was said to be a leader in the organization of black unions, with much of the credit going to Lide Meriwether.[65]

It was also Meriwether who led the Tennessee WCTU in the struggle to secure a prohibition amendment to the state consti-tution. Designed to eradicate both the sale and manufacture of liquor throughout the state, a referendum for such an amendment was held in 1887. Earlier efforts by temperance forces had focused on regulating only the sale of liquor. The Four Mile Law had been passed in 1877, making it unlawful to dispense intoxicating bev-erages within four miles of any chartered institution of learning outside an incorporated town. Towns that wanted to rid themselves of saloons surrendered their municipal status and obtained char-ters for schools. Within a few years of passage of the Four Mile Law, the retail liquor business had been prohibited in large areas of Tennessee.[66] Subsequent efforts to extend the law met resistance from the liquor interests, but temperance organizations were making headway convincing people that both the sale and manufacture of intoxicants in Tennessee should cease. The Order of the Good Templars, active in the state since the 1870s, the Prohibition Party, organized in Tennessee in 1883, and the WCTU were the most prominent groups working to influence public opinion in favor of complete prohibition.[67]

At the WCTU state convention in 1883 the women unequivocally declared their intention to use all of their resources to prevent the repeal of laws regulating liquor sales and "to secure through legislation the accomplishment of prohibition by submitting the question to the people at a time when no other issue is before them."[68]

As the temperance advocates mobilized for battle on behalf of a prohibition amendment, their first step was to get both the Republican and Democratic parties to include a prohibition referendum in their respective platforms. They then went to work campaigning throughout the state on behalf of candidates for the legislature who favored both the referendum idea and prohibition. Lide Meriwether, Elizabeth Saxon, and Mrs. M. L. Wells of Chattanooga covered the state delivering speeches and organizing new unions. The churches proved very receptive to the women's efforts, opening their doors as never before, and large and enthusiastic audiences gathered to listen. The number of new unions multiplied, days of prayer were observed, innumerable pieces of literature distributed, and the temperance women were described as being "in the heat of campaign work."[69] They were receiving invaluable training in the art and craft of politics, as they swarmed over the state and to the capitol in Nashville. In the legislative elections of 1886, most candidates who favored the prohibition referendum won, and a special election was subsequently scheduled for September 29, 1887.

The temperance women played a very visible role throughout this campaign. On election day they turned out in force, opened polling places with prayers, and "sweet women's voices" sang "'Hold the fort, for I am coming.' . . . Everywhere the women rallied, . . . Southern women who had been taught to believe that the polls were secret to men, and no woman's face should be seen on the street."[70]

In Memphis, women set up booths where they served coffee, sandwiches, and cakes while urging voters to support prohibition. There was "considerable demonstration" in the city on the issue, and the women were described as "very conspicuous." On election day, a crowd estimated at seven thousand gathered to hear speeches both for and against the proposed amendment.[71]

The amendment went down to defeat by a margin of some 17,000 votes. Antiprohibition sentiment was strongest in West Tennessee, and in Memphis 2,399 voted for prohibition while 6,821 were opposed.[72] But the WCTU leadership viewed their defeat as a lost battle in a long war that they were determined to win. While Memphis was referred to by temperance forces as a "small hell on the Mississippi,"[73] Memphis temperance women remained determined and saw the whole struggle as "war on the part of the Motherhood of Memphis for the home against the liquor traffic."[74]

The liquor interests were, however, a very formidable opponent. Memphis had long been noted as a wide-open river town where drinking and gambling flourished, and by the 1880s the city had become a liquor- and cigar-dealing center. Large liquor companies used Memphis as a warehousing depot from which to dispense their products into rural Mississippi, Arkansas, and Alabama. In addition, there was no dearth of local brewers and distillers. The liquor interests had become a strong factor in the city's economic makeup, generating income in the form of taxes, employment, and tourism. While many in the business community favored temperance and agreed that overindulgence led to many problems, they were against prohibition by legal statute.[75] These sentiments — also shared by the local press — when added to the clout of the liquor industry, provided sufficient support to block prohibition in 1887.

The decade following the defeat of that referendum represented a distinct trough in WCTU fortunes. Not all were quite as dedicated as the hard core, and there were defections. Lide Meriwether continued as president until 1897 and remained as committed as ever to winning prohibition in Tennessee, but the initiative shifted geographically to the eastern part of the state. All subsequent presidents of the Tennessee WCTU were from towns and cities in that region.

The state organization unwaveringly rededicated themselves to the goal of statewide prohibition, determined to "gather up the fragments shattered by the storm, lay them away and begin a new day."[76] They continued the work of influencing public opinion in favor of prohibition legislation, and by the turn of the century the WCTU seemed to be regaining its momentum. After the state convention of 1899, the number of unions began to grow and membership rose. The WCTU, in conjunction with the Anti-Saloon League, began to work for the extension of the Four Mile Law. They circulated petitions, initiated letter-writing campaigns to legislators, and lobbied at Nashville for legislation making the Four Mile Law more comprehensive. By 1901 saloons were abolished in all rural areas and in all but about sixty incorporated towns.[77] At the state WCTU convention in Columbia in 1907, a resolution was adopted stating that they considered Tennessee "now ready for absolute prohibition." For the next two years, "the gauntlet was down" as the women sent out thousands of letters and hundreds of thousands of pages of literature. Women speakers and workers traveled into every town and village, and petitions were widely circulated to present to the legislature thousands of names favoring prohibition.[78]

In the Democratic gubernatorial primary in 1908, the WCTU lined up behind E. Ward Carmack and his prohibition plank against the incumbent Governor Malcolm R. Patterson's local-option stand. Patterson, a Memphian, won the nomination and was reelected. Carmack was subsequently gunned down on the streets of Nashville by a friend of Patterson's, providing a martyr for the prohibition cause. Carmack's death was attributed to his zeal in opposing the liquor interests, thus dramatizing the need to rid the state of the evil liquor power. A memorial service was held in Memphis attended by an estimated crowd of some two thousand people. In eulogizing Carmack it was said: "He fell leading with knightly courage the forces that were battling in ridding Tennessee of its lawless elements and for absolute freedom from the domination of the saloon power, with all its resulting corruption, misery and crime."[79]

Carmack's murder intensified the prohibitionists' case, and when the Tennessee legislature convened in January 1909, consideration of a statewide prohibition bill was begun. All the temperance groups were extremely active, including the WCTU, which won endorsement from the Protestant Pastors Association. A number of Memphis churches held weekly meetings for the purpose of promoting the bill and issued regular public statements of support.[80]

On January 10, 1909, the prohibition bill was passed and Governor Patterson's veto overridden five days later. The temperance forces were elated, and the women in the gallery of the House sang the Doxology and later held religious services to give thanks.[81] However, the bill did not include an enforcement code. Thus officials not in sympathy with the new law did not enforce it, and Memphis was among the lax. Enforcement became the issue; and while measures to that end were passed in the legislature, the *Memphis Commercial Appeal* reported in 1917 that whiskey could still be had "in a hundred places" in Memphis.[82] Temperance supporters lamented circumvention of the statute in Memphis, and many citizens — even those who had opposed prohibition — joined the chorus demanding enforcement of the laws.

While Memphis was never "bone dry," the women had made their point. Whiskey was publicized as a great destroyer of home life and men's indulgence a clear sign of weakness. It was women's mission to arouse society to do its duty and stop the liquor trade in order to ensure happiness and prosperity in the homes of future generations.[83] Thus temperance spawned interest in a number of areas related to family well-being and stability, and contact among women throughout the state, as well as the nation, enhanced local awareness of the wide range of issues to which their energies could be applied. At the state WCTU convention in 1887 there were sixteen departments, each headed by a superintendent, which revealed the breadth of their undertakings.[84] In 1895 the work of the Memphis WCTU was described as evangelistic, educational, preventive, reformatory, social, and legal.[85] The WCTU provided the forum through which the women could disseminate information and organize public opinion in support of their efforts.

Throughout the decade of the 1890s and into the twentieth century, the temperance women — often in cooperation with other women's groups which had mushroomed into existence throughout the South at this time — initiated reforms that affected the lives of women and children. The Age of Consent Law is a case in point. Lide Meriwether had long been outspoken on the problem of prostitution and related issues, and she and Saxon played a leading role, via the Tennessee WCTU, in raising the age of consent in the state from ten to sixteen and later to eighteen years of age. Meriwether and Saxon raised the issue at WCTU meetings in Memphis, and support was subsequently organized throughout Tennessee via the temperance network. The topic was thought somewhat indelicate for public debate, but Saxon brushed aside such considerations pointing out that there was virtually no issue that could be considered inappropriately raised by "mothers," with the "sons of women."[86]

It was the WCTU which succeeded in 1895 in winning passage of a Scientific Temperance Instruction Law, requiring the teaching of the effects of alcohol and narcotics on the human system in all state-supported schools. The fourth Friday in October was also set aside as Frances Willard Day in public schools, and programs on the evils of intemperance were presented. Temperance women invaded the jails, asylums, poorhouses, and hospitals, directing their attention to the women housed there and broadening their own knowledge of social conditions while focusing society's attention upon the needs and interests peculiar to women and children in an increasingly urban atmosphere. Temperance women became the champions of the underdog and entered the lists on behalf of the indigent and helpless.

Following the approach taken by the national organization earlier, the Memphis temperance group in 1885 moved toward endorsement of woman suffrage as a means of achieving political, economic, and social equality for women.[87] Largely at the prodding of Lide Meriwether, the Memphis WCTU voted unanimously to add a suffrage plank to its platform and created a franchise department to carry on that work. For the next two years, Meriwether and Elizabeth Saxon worked diligently writing letters, making speeches, and traveling in Tennessee on behalf of woman suffrage.[88]

The women were finding it extremely frustrating and maddening to be politely heard and politely ignored. When the WCTU got a bill introduced into the Tennessee legislature in 1887 requesting that a woman physician be appointed for female patients in the insane hospital, the legislators' response was astonishment. "Such an innovation had never entered the brain of our Southern chivalry," commented the temperance women, as the bill was voted down.[89] And after the defeat of the prohibition referendum in 1887, WCTU activists pointed out that if women had been casting ballots instead of handing out cakes and sandwiches, the results might well have been different. Shortly after that defeat the *Union Signal* commented: "Not to demand suffrage and yet to exercise all that makes suffrage a power, is clearly absurd. The right to stand at the polls and solicit votes carries with it the right to vote. If one is permissible the other must be, and women who exercise one will at last insist on the other."[90]

When Lide Meriwether left for Nashville to attend the Prohibition Party's convention in 1888, her husband urged her to win a woman suffrage plank "or," he said, "we will never have girlhood protected nor equal wages, nor equal work, nor just legislation for women in anything until women can legislate."[91]

Some Memphis women such as the Meriwethers and Saxons had long believed in the justice of voting rights for women but recognized the difficulty of garnering grass-roots support in a southern community. The temperance issue had provided the wedge by which the idea of suffrage could be successfully promoted. Via temperance, women could act aggressively and assertively in directing society, without fear of opposition from male relatives. In her role as protector of the home and family, woman's zeal was regarded as admirable rather than misplaced. The WCTU allowed women a means by which to bridge the gap between womanly concerns and demands for equality.

While "home protection" remained the dominant justification for the female franchise among Memphis women well into the second decade of the twentieth century, by 1914 the argument from natural rights was being increasingly heard. At a suffrage rally in Court Square in 1914, one speaker said that freedom should be women's — "they deserved it as a right and also as an opportunity for greater service."[92] The following year at the same May Day suffrage rally, Mrs. Harry B. Anderson said that no man could stop the movement, "because it meant justice."[93] The female franchise was no longer the radical cause it had once seemed to many Memphis women. In the thirty-five years from its adoption by the Memphis WCTU to the ratification of the Nineteenth Amendment in 1920, women's attitude toward their political participation had evolved from one of vacillation and doubt to one of certitude and conviction. They had become confident about their ability to initiate change and possessed a much clearer vision of how to achieve those goals.

Barbara Epstein has called the WCTU "profeminist" because of its focus on women's interests and advocacy of the franchise as a means of achieving female equality.[94] Ruth Bordin also described the WCTU as "feminist" in that its members, in pursuit of temperance goals, took control of their own lives as well as responsibility for the society in which they lived.[95] The positions of these two historians are largely borne out in the case of the temperance women in Memphis in the late nineteenth century. They felt their influence growing as they stepped into a part of the world previously closed to them. The cause of temperance, in its versatility, had greatly expanded public access for women. There was a clear linkage between temperance and suffrage, temperance education in schools, prisons, and the whole range of public institutions, and the need for women to serve on school boards as well as the boards of charitable institutions. Women became comfortable expressing themselves on secular matters, and their confidence in their own abilities and opinions on public issues grew. When Meriwether, Saxon, and Wells spoke before the Tennessee legislature in favor of prohibition, it was "the first time that women's voices had ever been heard in those halls . . . and common justice forced the hearers to admit that the three women of the WCTU could be both logical and eloquent."[96] At the state Temperance Alliance Convention in 1887, when Wells objected to the wording of a resolution and it was subsequently amended, Meriwether commented: "Think how it would have sounded ten years ago, to say that, in a public convention, a woman objected to a resolution and 478 men went to work, and amended the resolution to suit her. Verily, 'the world do move'!"[97]

The temperance issue, which women could so clearly relate to their duty as defenders of the family, marked another vital step toward nascent sisterhood through united action. In Memphis, women's social activism reached very nearly explosive proportions in the decade of the 1890s, and the WCTU had played an important role in this evolution.

4

The Nineteenth Century Club

With the arrival of the women's club movement in Memphis the mainstream joined the social-reform bandwagon. The Women's Christian Association and Woman's Christian Temperance Union, together with the efforts of a number of individuals, had created an awareness of the many difficulties — particularly for women and children — of urban living. The political, legal, and economic disabilities under which women lived were increasingly apparent, and organizations such as the WCA and WCTU had provided a collective means through which these problems could be addressed, once identified. The knowledge of Memphis women about female reform activities in other parts of the country had also grown as a result of membership in these groups, providing additional encouragement for further involvement. In working together to achieve their goals, the evolution of a sisterhood among elite, white women of Memphis continued to develop, reaching full flower with the club movement.

The development of women's clubs in late nineteenth-century Memphis was an important step in the formation of a distinctly "female world" which Carroll Smith-Rosenberg has called the "creation of women."[1] It was a world characterized by mutual support, companionship, female alliances, and the growth of a shared vision of what society should be. Collectively, club women created a formidable energy and versatility. There was a wide variety of women's clubs organized in Memphis in the 1890s, and by 1895 it was estimated that the city had some forty literary, educational, and philanthropic organizations, not including religious associations connected with church work. Most were begun for literary and cultural purposes, but within a year or two their attention, in varying degrees, often turned to community projects.[2] The Nineteenth Century Club was the largest and most influential, occupying a dominant and pivotal position in the life of Memphis club women in the late nineteenth and early twentieth centuries.

In the spring of 1890 a small group of elite, white women in Memphis formed a club dedicated to the intellectual development of women, which would become one of the South's foremost female organizations. Elise Massey Selden was the catalyst.[3] She had returned to Memphis from a trip to New York City where she had visited a woman's club and was very much excited by the activity she had seen.[4] She assembled a group of acquaintances that became the nucleus of the Nineteenth Century Club. Somewhat doubtful about how the concept of a woman's club would be received in Memphis, Selden suggested that the president should be a woman of impeccable social credentials. Thus Mrs. Robert C. Brinkley was asked to become the first president. She was described as "a leader of Memphis society,"[5] and her husband was among the foremost powers in the business community.[6]

The women felt confident that Mrs. Brinkley's presidency, plus fifteen charter members of solid respectability, would blunt any negative response.[7] The very word *club* in relation to women was said to have bad connotations, particularly to the minds of men, who feared that the appearance of women's clubs would lead them to abandon home duties.[8] One member of the Nineteenth Century Club, Sarah Beaumont Kennedy, also noted some opposition because the "old southern notion of women courting publicity was deemed improper."[9]

Nevertheless, in early May 1890, a meeting of some eighty women was held at the Gayoso Hotel, where the name Nineteenth Century Club was chosen and a constitution and by-laws written. The response was very positive, and the women were filled with enthusiasm for their project. Convinced that the club would be for the "permanent good of the community," they proclaimed, "At last Memphis has an organization of her women, which is so comprehensive and at the same time within such wise limits, that great good must be the result."[10]

Elise Massey Selden. A native Memphian, Elise Massey Selden had been a founding member of the Thackeray Book Club, the Free Kindergarten Association and the Memphis Suffrage Association. In 1890, she initiated the founding of the Nineteenth Century Club, dedicated to the intellectual development of women. (Courtesy of the Nineteenth Century Club.)

That the women remained somewhat skeptical about the general public reaction to the formation of their club is revealed in their phrase *wise limits*. The Nineteenth Century Club's constitution stated clearly that their objectives were to promote the female intellect by encouraging "a spirit of research in literary fields and provide an intellectual center for the women of Memphis."[11] Social approval was an important factor determining their behavior, and they seemed intent on making assurances that their intention was not to usurp functions deemed unsuitable for women. Anticipating that a woman's club might elicit a certain amount of anxiety, they were careful about their actions and statements. Florence Turner, who was among the earliest members and remained active in club affairs throughout her life, said of the club's purpose:

> It is not an attempt to dictate to city officials how they shall perform the duties of their office. Neither is there the slightest tinge of politics connected with the movement. . . . To improve civic pride, to elevate civic ideals, that is the purpose of this movement. The individual citizen is the all important factor in the work which our club has undertaken to perform. Of course, there is room for certain improvements in this city, else there would have been no germ for this movement.[12]

Main Street, Memphis, circa 1900. The Gayoso Hotel was the site of the founding of the Nineteenth Century Club in May 1890. (Courtesy of the West Tennessee Historical Society.)

Despite Turner's disclaimer regarding political intentions and the constitution's statement about educational purposes, it was clear that the women did intend to become involved in politics. "Philanthropy and Reform" was among the four committees formed by the club in 1891.[13] Under the guise of municipal housekeeping and the promotion of citizenship, the women attempted to influence city officials in carrying out the duties of their respective offices. The Nineteenth Century Club gradually developed a vision of what its members wanted Memphis to become—a vibrant, people-filled city, which included parks, schools, hospitals, asylums, and playgrounds. They wanted to participate in the development of their fast-growing city and believed it incumbent upon women to actively engage in moral, philanthropic, and educational projects. They believed it important to inject women's "gentler spirit," their "more loving wisdom," into the planning and running of municipal affairs. "Without the uplifting influence of women civilization itself would become material, even brutal. . . . The advancemet of women in the eternal scheme of things, means the advancement of the race," they stated.[14]

Their hopes were similar to those that women in the North and East had been working to realize for some years — to make women first aware of abuses in a male-dominated society, particularly as they affected women and children, and then to politicize their grievances by actively purusing improvement.[15] The appearance of the Nineteenth Century Club in 1890 was a clear indication that southern women, specifically these women of Memphis, were ready to seize the initiative to pursue projects and perform duties that required activism in the public sphere.

The contagion of women's clubs in the 1890s was noted at the time by a local club woman who commented that women seemed "peculiarly sensitive" to the influence of clubs and had responded to the club idea "with much greater enthusiasm than men." Clubs were viewed as schools where women were "stimulated to go to the very edge of her possibilities . . . propelled . . . to new intellectual heights." The commentator, Annah Robinson Watson, a founding member and third president of the Nineteenth Century Club, also cautioned women to keep their public activities in their proper context, being careful not "to seek to gratify an unreasoning ambition. By this sin fell the angels." Watson expressed the sentiments of most of her contemporaries when she said that a woman's first loyalty and responsibility was to her own home:

> It is best for her, best for her husband and children, that her interests be broad and Catholic; but not that outside interests absorb too large a share of her attention. . . . No woman has a right to bring to her home a devitalized personality. She has no right to bestow her best elsewhere and bring to her home, her husband and children, the wearied and exhausted personality which is left.[16]

Ever sensitive to criticism, the Memphis women were careful to point out that theirs was a very selfless and therefore very female brand of activism. As expressed by the Nineteenth Century Club membership: "Achievement for the sake of prominence and prestige has never been a Club objective. . . . Literally, it seems, the un-written law of the Club and its membership has been 'much can be accomplished if we are not concerned about who gets the rec-ognition.'"[17] Self-sacrifice, service to others, and female responsi-bility for the home were points invariably recited when the topic of women's clubs was discussed. Nineteenth Century Club women remained defensive about their activities, and after almost a dec-ade continued to feel the necessity of excusing the club's existence by explaining how membership made a woman "an ideal help-meet to her husband," a "better companion" to both spouse and children.[18]

Nevertheless, as Clara Conway expressed it, the women were ready to "enter the world," and Annah Robinson Watson noted a "new sense of power and capacity among American women."[19] The Nineteenth Century Club motto, "Influence is Responsibility," epito-mized their newly revealed feelings of accountability for the future direction of society. In 1892 when the Congress of the Association for the Advancement of Women assembled for its twentieth annual meeting at the Nineteenth Century Club—the first time the organ-ization had ever met in a southern city—Conway made the opening remarks.[20] She said Memphis women wanted to "enter the circle of its earnest work and share its high privileges." The time had come, she said, to "move away from self-ease" and to forget leisure, to "give up the kingdom of the past to hear and heed and answer the 'Cry of the World.'" Women, said Conway, "were impatient with incompleteness."[21]

The Nineteenth Century Club was a success from the start. In its first year membership had more than doubled. It is probable that part of the appeal of the Nineteenth Century Club lay in its aura of social elitism, since membership would certainly have reas-sured aspiring elites of their haute bourgeois status. As one historian has commented, a plutocracy had arisen in Memphis, self-made, and they wanted to show it off. "One's wife joined the Nineteenth Century Club where she became a 'new woman' by studying village life in India and Egyptology."[22] Another, somewhat less denigrat-ing depiction of the Nineteenth Century Club was that it was basi-cally an innocuous auxiliary to the mainstream of economic development.[23] Implicit in both views is the opinion that the existence of the Nineteenth Century Club did not affect the fortunes of the city of Memphis in any very crucial way. Such interpretations largely ignore the public contributions of the club and completely overlook the organization as an indicator of change within a developing female community. The Nineteenth Century Club filled a widely felt need for many of the city's women by providing a channel for their intellectual yearnings and a vehicle through which they could implement their ideas about the direction of the city's growth. There was a distinct sense of urgency and vibrancy among these women, as though they felt themselves poised on the brink of a new beginning — which indeed they were.

Yet the Nineteenth Century Club was, by national standards, a tardy entry in the woman's club field. Women's clubs for social and secular purposes had made their earliest appearance in the North and East in the 1860s. Jane Cunningham Croly's Sorosis, organized in New York City in 1868, is generally said to be a prototype. The spark for Sorosis was the exclusion of women from the Press Club's dinner party honoring Charles Dickens, although Croly says women were "hungry for the society of women . . . for the society of those whose deeper natures had been arosed to activity, who had been seized by the divine spirit of inquiry and aspiration, who were interested in the thought and progress of the age and in what other women were thinking and doing."[24]

Along with gibes, sneers, and much ridicule, came predictions of an early death for the club; instead, Sorosis foreshadowed a trend, and women's clubs dedicated to literary and self-help pursuits became a widespread phenomenon. The Nineteenth Century Club came into existence at a time when these established women's organizations were shifting their emphasis away from literary pursuits and toward community reform. Municipal housekeeping moved to center stage throughout the 1870s, 80s, and 90s, becoming the advance guard of the women's club movement. The women increasingly made it their main business to inject into society their idea of what a reasonable government should provide.

Elise Selden's presence in New York City in 1890 and her subsequent initiative in founding the Nineteenth Century Club established a link between the Memphis club movement and the ferment occurring in the East.[25] While the Ossoli Circle of Knoxville predated the Nineteenth Century Club by five years, and it is certain that Memphis women were aware of Ossoli's existence, available evidence indicates that it was Selden's New York experience that prompted the Nineteenth Century Club's founding. However, as has been noted, the Nineteenth Century Club was hesitant about plunging too aggressively and openly into civic affairs. They began cautiously, somewhat behind the more progressive elements within the national women's club setting. While municipal housekeeping would be a very important part of the Nineteenth Century Club's identity, the Memphis women sustained an interest in literary pursuits later than northern and eastern clubs, where the cultural emphasis was becoming obsolete.

Immediately following its initial organizational gatherings, the Nineteenth Century Club rented a room in downtown Memphis[26] and began holding biweekly meetings, which consisted of programs sponsored by the various committees, with papers presented by the members themselves. Early club agendas indicate a methodical investigation of women in all fields of work—almost a crash course of information about women's life and activities. The committees focused on women in literature, music, art, education, domestic life, and reform activities. There was a large task of self-education before them, both to gain knowledge of what other women were doing and to provide some basis upon which to determine their own future course of action. They addressed themselves to urban life on a very broad front and through their committees offered something that could accommodate the developing interests of practically every woman. Toward the late 1890s, their focus was increasingly upon civic reform.

Shortly after the turn of the century, club president Florence Turner commented that the Nineteenth Century Club deserved much credit for inaugurating the civic improvement movement in Memphis, and upon it, she believed, would also depend much of that movement's success. Members had also succeeded in winning wide approval for the woman's club idea and had largely overcome the initial hesitancy of many—both men and women. Commented Mattie

Jones, president of the Nineteenth Century Club for 1901 to 1902: "If there are any women who don't approve of clubs, I feel they have missed something in life by not knowing the Nineteenth Century Club. The gentlemen all approve of us and are ready helpers in time of need. . . . The things we do together are things that move the world."[27]

Unity was considered essential as a major means to power and became an important objective of women's clubs nationally, as well as on the state and local levels. From their earliest days, club women had attempted to promote a united womanhood by bringing into the movement a large constituency. Jane Cunningham Croly and Sorosis spearheaded the formation of a Woman's Parliament in 1868, and when that foundered they initiated the Association for the Advancement of Women. This latter group eventually was superseded by the General Federation of Women's Clubs, organized in the spring of 1890 in New York City. Their motto, "Unity in Diversity," reflected the federation concept, which became enormously successful in facilitating cooperation and collaboration among women's clubs all over the country while allowing wide latitude on the local level. National headquarters sent out speakers, circulated information on issues important to women, and held annual conventions at which women from all sections came together and shared ideas. Unity of thought and action and female camaraderie were greatly enhanced, and the unity concept was widely emphasized and encouraged.[28]

In Memphis a city-wide network of club women materialized in 1893 with the formation of the Woman's Council, a direct outgrowth of the meeting of the Association for the Advancement of Women, which had been held the previous year at the Nineteenth Century Club's headquarters. Mary Jamison Judah, Clara Conway, and Mrs. Carrington Mason, all Nineteenth Century Club members, pursued the idea of establishing an organization which would "bind all clubs together and give unanimity of purpose to all."[29] Within a few years, the Woman's Council had evolved into a clearinghouse and liaison among the rapidly expanding women's club movement, helping to focus and unite the women of the city for more effective action. By 1895 the Woman's Council had a membership of forty-eight organizations encompassing over three thousand

Some Nineteenth Century Club Members in 1904. *Seated, left to right*: Mrs. Lewis Donelson, Mrs. Napoleon Hill, Mrs. C.N. Grosvenor, Mrs. Alston Boyd, Mrs. Kate Trader Barrow, Mrs. Laura Neblett, Mrs. J.L. Minor. *Standing, first row, left to right*: Mrs. Levi Joy, Mrs. A.M. Austin, Mrs. T.B. Andrews, Mrs. Mary Beecher, Mrs. Fred Anderson, Mrs. Neely Grant, Miss Frances Church, Mrs. M.E. Carter, Mrs. Andrew Donelson, Mrs. Charles Cole, Mrs. Samuel McCallum, Mrs. Brooks Hachett. *Standing, second row*: Miss Mary Hill Overton, Mrs. Phoebe Evans, Mrs. R.P. Woodson. (Courtesy of the West Tennessee Historical Society Collection.)

women. They held monthly meetings at which representatives from the member organizations reported on their work, made appeals for collaboration on specific projects, and devised strategies for carrying out their undertakings. Their motto, "All for Each, Each for All," reflected the recurring and dominant philosophy of cooperation — with the Woman's Council providing the vehicle through which local cooperation and communication could be accomplished.[30]

On the heels of the success of this local effort came the formation of the Tennessee Federation of Women's Clubs in 1896 at the initiative of the Knoxville club, Ossoli Circle.[31] The state federation provided the same type of coordination among the clubs of Tennessee as the national group did for a wider area and pledged its members "to strive for better homes, schools, lives, surroundings, scholarships, civic health and righteousness, the conservation of forests and places of natural beauty, and protection for unfortunate children and women laborers."[32]

From 20 clubs initially affiliated in Tennessee, the number had increased to 157 by 1915, 9 of which were Memphis clubs. Mrs. J. M. Greer, president of the Nineteenth Century Club in 1895, had chaired the organizational meeting of the Tennessee Federation of Women's Clubs, and Mrs. W. D. Beard, also a member of the Nineteenth Century Club, was elected first president of the state organization. The Nineteenth Century Club would continue to play an active role in the planning and execution of many of the federation's projects, which offered new fields of endeavor and expanded scope for women's ever-widening ambitions.[33]

The Nineteenth Century Club members were constantly identifying problems and bringing them to the attention of authorities, local or state. If an appropriate government department did not exist, they lobbied for the creation of one. There was no set procedure, as they had little experience in public affairs, and trial and error tended to be their modus operandi. While not doctrinaire, the Nineteenth Century Club did hope to inspire others with what were considered the responsibilities of citizenship. They were concerned that their husbands and other male relatives allowed themselves to become too immersed in the process of "money-getting." While on the one hand they wanted to coax women out of their hesitancy about participating in civic affairs, on the other they attempted to impress upon men the harmful imprint that callous materialism could have upon the city's future. These club women wanted to achieve a sense of "community life" in Memphis, which they believed required an individual to recognize "his obligation to society as well as his privileges."[34] They hoped for cooperation between the sexes in improving the city, and on several occasions made concerted efforts to enlist male participation.

In 1892 for example, largely through the urging of the women of the city, the legislative council addressed the issues of widespread violations of the liquor laws and the openness and prevalence of gambling and prostitution.[35] "In these attempts at moral cleaning up women were not idle. They urged their husbands, fathers, brothers, sons and friends on in the work and they themselves came forward in a public way more than ever before in Memphis history."[36]

Out of this protest grew the Law and Order League, a male organization whose membership reflected the same families as the rolls of the Nineteenth Century Club.[37] Its formation was primarily the result of women calling attention to problems and urging men to act. As Florence Turner pointed out, "A little agitation . . . is the beginning of all progress."[38] The focus of this group was on the enforcement of existing laws and expulsion of corrupt officeholders. Its emphasis on providing "clean government" was characteristic of the progressive thrust of that era, and the organization provided an example of one aspect of structural progressivism at work in Memphis. Law and Order League investigations led to the disbarment of a prominent lawyer for dishonest and unprofessional conduct, the impeachment and expulsion of a judge, and indictments by the Shelly County Grand Jury of 225 unlicensed dispensers of "red eye."

By the turn of the century, as it became more commonplace to see women participating in public activities, there was greater integration of the sexes in reform endeavors and the breadth of interest also expanded. The women were succeeding in bringing men into areas of social reform. The Civic Progress League, formed in 1908, provides an excellent example.

The Civic Progress League was an organization whose purpose was to improve "general conditions" in Memphis and included male and female members. It was a direct outgrowth of the all-female Housekeepers' Club, which expanded into "an organization having a broader scope of usefulness with increased membership."[39] The Housekeepers' Club was begun in 1895 by Minnie Walter Myers, a Nineteenth Century Club member who had served on the first Philanthropy and Reform Committee.[40] Myers was deeply interested in promoting domestic science and organized the Housekeepers' Club in order to bring women together for "the intelligent study of home and its requirements," and to make the "machinery of the household work more smoothly,"[41] Through the years the club's interests widened, and by 1907 its scope was described as "immense, embracing almost every subject which pertains to the general welfare."[42] The Housekeepers' Club established an employment bureau to find jobs for young women, brought about the introduction of domestic science into the public school curriculum, organized public play-schools for very young children, and focused attention upon the need for municipal aesthetics.[43]

The enlargement of the Housekeepers' Club into the Civic Progress League in 1908 came at the initiative of women led by Minnie Myers. The inclusion of men increased their membership pool, and the committees indicated interest in a wide range of areas: civic beautification, sanitary conditions, tuberculosis control, general public hygiene, home environment, and a children's welfare department. They made a point of stressing that their purpose was "not social,"[44] as though such assurance was needed to underscore their seriousness since men and women would be working together. L. B. McFarland, who had played an important role in establishing the Park Commission in Memphis in 1899 and had served as its first chairman, became head of the Civic Progress League's Civic Improvement committee. One of the city's social and business elite,[45] McFarland brought to the league an already distinguished record of public service, backed by his belief in the necessity of aesthetics to the growth and progress of any city. In McFarland's view, "Our municipal government must catch this spirit of progress and respond to the demands of the occasion by providing us with public parks commensurate with the growth and greatness of our city. Every consideration of health, need and pride demand these; and at any price."[46]

The impact of such men as McFarland—and other male officers and committee heads equally as prominent in other fields—as partners in the league, provides evidence of a well-orchestrated plan on the part of Minnie Myers and her female cohorts.[47] The interests of these men and women dovetailed nicely, but it was the women's organizational initiative that assured the continued development of these areas into institutional permanence. The Nineteenth Century Club, whose tentacles had reached out to found the Housekeepers' Club, had in turn spawned the Civic Progress League.

It is probable that Myers's experience with organized womanhood through the Nineteenth Century Club influenced her decision to establish the Housekeepers' Club. It was characteristic of the Nineteenth Century Club to encourage civic endeavors even though there might be overlapping interests. There were no "pet" projects jealously guarded. On the contrary, club members strove to promote concentration in a specific area—as evidenced by Myers and her group. As the club expressed it: "This Club wears no prouder title than to have been called 'A Clearing House of Good Ideas.' Whenever an organization wishes to specialize and is better equipped to do the work, the Club gladly surrenders an established activity and sends it forth with its good wishes and blessing."[48]

Sincerely altruistic, these women were genuinely dedicated to promoting any group that was believed to be acting in the best interests of society. They were dedicated to the principle of cooperation, and while undoubtedly reveling in new opportunities to express their own personal ambitions, they encouraged activities that they believed would work for the benefit of all. The Housekeepers' Club, for example, brought more women into the fold of working together to provide additional opportunities for even larger numbers of women—which was an ultimate objective of club women.

There was also frequent cooperation between the Nineteenth Century Club and other civic organizations where interests coincided. They joined forces with the Civic Progress League for its Municipal Cleaning Day, in which special attention was focused upon cleaning unsightly vacant lots and alleys.[49] There were also joint efforts with the Businessmen's Club, later the Chamber of Commerce. Often the men's group asked for a delegation from the Nineteenth Century Club to meet and discuss a particular problem. Requests from the men to the women usually involved social matters, such as entertaining visitors to Memphis, organizing a charity ball, or publicizing a program of the chamber.[50] However, there was cooperation on more substantive matters. For example, the Nineteenth Century Club and Chamber of Commerce protested to the county court about appropriations for a new jail, the club members preferring the detention-farm idea, which they considered more "forward looking." Another example of meaningful cooperation was when the Health Department of the Nineteenth Century Club successfully enlisted support from the business community in backing a bill to secure a tuberculosis hospital in Memphis.[51] With membership approaching one thousand by 1921, the women of the Nineteenth Century Club described themselves as "a big pulsing force in Memphis — equal in power to the Chamber of Commerce in many things and equally necessary in the progressive life of Memphis."[52]

The Nineteenth Century Club was also conspicuous in its support of other women's groups, playing an important role in bringing many women's organizations together for united action to support reform. The need for a police matron is a case in point and is illustrative of the type of cooperation developing among the women of the city. For some time there had been concern expressed about the care of women prisoners, and in 1897 a meeting was held at the Nineteenth Century Club attended by representatives from several women's organizations to discuss the need for a police matron. Mrs. Elise Selden, president of the club, related unsuccessful efforts of both the Women's Christian Association and the Woman's Council to secure the establishment of such an office. As Lide Meriwether, who had been involved in the earlier efforts, explained, the city administration had maintained that as female prisoners in the South were predominantly black, there could be little hope that a matron could turn them to better ways. In addition, officials had insisted that no self-respecting white woman would take on such a job. Meriwether then presented a report from the police matron at Knoxville,

Mrs. E. C. Wright, who was described as "a refined and womanly woman." Mrs. Wright's report stated that her work in Knoxville had succeeded beyond her most "sanguine expectations," and that "Woman's Work for Woman" was going forward there with much hope. "I think all prejudice will be removed when it is properly understood," she said. "The strongest reason I can give for the appointment of a police matron is this: There is no situation in life in which woman can be placed where she does not need the counsel, sympathy and friendship of her sister woman. A police matron is the friend of every unfortunate woman with whom she comes in contact."[53] Mrs. Wright reported dealing with some 1,609 cases in one year—Lide Meriwether being quick to point out that Knoxville was only about one-third as large as Memphis. Clearly, said Meriwether, there would be a great deal of work for a Memphis matron.[54]

A Woman's Christian Temperance Union member commented that despite claims of the mayor and chief of police that women were never locked up at the police station, her own personal obserations of the actual situation were quite different. She stated:

> The mayor told me the other day that there never had been a woman locked up in the police station since he had been mayor. I have been in the prison. I have seen women, white and colored, locked in the cells. I have talked to them there. . . . Now, these gentlemen do not know what goes on about their station-house, or they are telling fairy stories.[55]

Elizabeth Saxon urged women to bring all their influence to bear upon their male relatives. She maintained that "where the women of a city are in earnest about a matter they can usually bring it about."[56] The women decided to circulate petitions throughout the city and present them to the city council, in addition to continuing their meetings at the Nineteenth Century Club for further discussion of the question.

There was also cooperation between black and white women on the police matron issue. Julia Hooks, a black woman who had been involved in jail work, addressed a meeting held at the Nineteenth Century Club and thanked those women for the movement they had launched. Clearly the sense of the meeting was that the work was for the benefit of all women, and Hooks's remarks were said to have been "warmly applauded."[57] The city administration, a male bastion, represented a barrier to be crossed, and there was a definite sense of women, regardless of color, cooperating to achieve their goal. It may well have been because of Elizabeth Saxon and Lide Meriwether that blacks and whites were brought together on this matter. It was these two "comrades in arms," who had first encouraged black-white cooperation in Memphis in the temperance crusade. Thus, transcending race in the interest of problems common to their gender was not a new idea to Memphis women, and the meeting of blacks and whites together did not seem unusual.

In the weeks and months just prior to the mayoral election of 1898, the club women of Memphis held "meetings without number" lobbying for a police matron. At one mass meeting at the Nineteenth Century Club, a letter from candidate J. J. Williams had been read expressing his support for their idea.[58] Williams won the election, and before the end of February a city police matron had been appointed. One woman active in the campaign said that Williams's election "was really due to the work of the women, who promised him the office if he would give them the matron."[59] Indeed Elizabeth Saxon's comment about women's influence may have hit the mark. It is impossible to know exactly how much impact the women had, but family and social connections would undoubtedly have given them the opportunity to bring pressure to bear upon men prominent in business and political affairs. In any event, following Williams's election there was an "avalanche" of applications for the matron's position. The new mayor explained he would follow the recommendation of the women, and when the Woman's Council and the Nineteenth Century Club endorsed M. Elizabeth Roark for the job, she was appointed.[60]

The women had been determined to succeed in getting a police matron, and the Nineteenth Century Club had provided an effective forum. Past failures by other women's groups had only sparked their resolve and realization of the need for more united action. The idea of an office of police matron initially had been regarded as very experimental and a great innovation, and Roark's report of her first year's work reveals that she did a great deal more than search arrested females. She dispensed medicine and clothing to hundreds of prisoners, arranged for hospital stays, placed young girls in the Women's Christian Association Refuge and Home of the Good Shepherd, helped some find employment, arranged a marriage, and attempted to deal with all the problems and misery attendant upon broken homes, deserted wives, and helpless children. The *Memphis Commercial Appeal* editorialized: "The creation of the office of police matron in Memphis was a recognition of the plea for the reforming of the criminal; and the work done during the last nine months amply vindicates the wisdom of those humane women who insisted on the necessity of establishing such an office."[61] On this issue the women had pressed and won, the advantages of their idea receiving almost instant recognition.

Another municipal office that found its way into women's hands was that of sanitary inspector for the Board of Health. Behind the idea was the Department of Philanthropy of the Nineteenth Century Club, led in 1909 by Grace Smith and Sarah Beaumont Kennedy,[62] whose committee had cooperated with the city's Board of Health on a variety of projects.[63] The job of sanitary inspector had been held by a male doctor, but the gathering sentiment was that he could give only a limited amount of time to city duties, whereas a woman would be able to devote full time to the job.[64] At the March 1909 meeting of the fire and police commissioners, Dr. Andrews explained that he wanted a woman for the job of sanitary inspector because, he argued, "There are many stores and factories where conditions can only be viewed by a woman."[65] The following month, Mrs. E. C. Mooney, widow of prominent businessman David C. Mooney and candidate of the Nineteenth Century Club, was appointed sanitary inspector of the Board of Health.[66]

With the appointment of Mrs. Mooney there was a shift of focus toward the needs of employees and the often shocking conditions under which they labored. As J. P. Young pointed out: "Many Memphis employers, like those in other parts of the world, grow in prosperity without considering the comfort or convenience of those who are assisting in their business growth, unless forced to do so."[67] The women of Memphis in this case "forced them to do so." By the end of the year, Mooney had made impressive inroads and publicized the often deplorable conditions she discovered. She had found "numerous kitchens" and places "not so apt to be discovered by men," which she ordered cleaned and kept clean, and played an important role in enforcing pure food laws.[68] Dr. Andrews commented: "This inspectress had unearthed conditions in factories and stores where women are employed and in other places which are almost impossible to believe."[69]

The issue of female competence had not appeared in the discussions surrounding the choice of sanitary inspector—in marked contrast to some of the male commentary of prior decades. In the intervening years, women's increased public activities and civic presence had provided evidence of female abilities, establishing their right to public participation.

About the time Mrs. Mooney's revelations were being brought to light, the Nineteenth Century Club turned its attention to the tuberculosis problem in Memphis—a disease the women hoped to see eradicated. It was a leading cause of death and was of great concern to health officials. At Nineteenth Century Club meetings the membership was advised of widespread unsanitary conditions in the city, and in 1908 the Civic Improvement Department adopted a resolution to send a committee to confer with city council members about the problem. In that same year the club was responsible for a tuberculosis exhibit in Memphis which received much coverage and special acknowledgment from the Board of Health.[70] The women of the Nineteenth Century Club believed it was their job "to arouse the public to the need of each individual's help in the sanitation of our city,"—which they viewed as a requirement of good citizenship.[71] They believed an informed public would bring action, and in 1916 when the Memphis and Shelby County Anti-Tuberculosis Society was formed to act as a "clearinghouse" between citizens and patients at the tuberculosis hospital, the women received much credit. The following year the legislature passed a bill providing for a new hospital, and the Nineteenth Century Club's Health Department again received acknowledgment for inspiring the public sentiment necessary for passage.[72]

Women increasingly regarded health and sanitation as a female province and dedicated themselves to the creation of a sanitary and healthful environment for citizens. When women spoke of health as "largely a woman's problem," they meant it in the municipal-housekeeping sense of being accountable for the "broader home, the community in which they live and bring up their children."[73] The Nineteenth Century Club women were forceful and intrepid in invading the public sphere in areas they believed were a rightful extension of "home duties," but they showed no interest in invading the medical profession. There were a few female medical doctors in Memphis in the early twentieth century, and available information — which is very sketchy — indicates they were a part of the developing women's community.[74] While the club women of Memphis were generally admiring and accepting of female doctors, referring to one as "very popular" and another as proof of high intellect in women,[75] the encouragement of young women into the medical profession never became a club objective. The attention of club women was mainly focused on projects to promote health within their own households and the "household" of the community.

In its efforts at rooting out tuberculosis, the Civic Improvement Department of the Nineteenth Century Club had undertaken a systematic investigation of city sanitation in 1913 — surveying alleys and vacant lots, checking into housing problems and the general conditions affecting health — and found much that was both unsanitary and unsightly.[76] Their discoveries, which had contributed to the developing sentiment for action against tuberculosis, also prompted a city-beautiful campaign led by Mrs. A. B. DeLoach, chairman of the Civic Improvement Department, and her committee.[77] The women emphasized the need for attention to aesthetics and sponsored a floral market where flowers and shrubbery were sold at low prices, raising money that in turn was awarded as prizes for the best flower-box window, yard garden, and factory garden. The appearance of a permanent Flower Mart and the spread of backyard gardens were also the work of the club women, and the *Memphis Commercial Appeal* reminded citizens that while the Park Commission and Rotarians had played a role in the city-beautiful effort, "we must not forget that the first practical work was done along these lines by the good ladies of the Nineteenth Century Club."[78]

The achievement of many of their objectives required legislation, and by the early twentieth century women were becoming a common sight in legislative halls. They were influential in winning new laws largely affecting women and children, as well as achieving for themselves the right to an increased number of public offices. At the 1898 convention of the Tennessee Federation of Women's Clubs, held in Chattanooga, Elise Selden, representing the Nineteenth Century Club, presented the draft of a bill proposing the eligibility of women to serve on school boards in Tennessee. Selden's proposal dovetailed with another project of the Tennessee Federation of Women's Clubs, which was the establishment of a vocational reformatory for girls. For a woman to be superintendent of the new institution and to serve on its board of managers required an act of the legislature. In 1915 the Eligibility of Women on Boards bill was signed into law, giving women the right to serve on boards of education in cities and counties and on governing boards of state, county, and municipal institutions.[79] It had taken almost two decades to accomplish this goal, during which time there was a continuous presence of women in the legislature — lobbying committees and attending legislative sessions — activities which the women described as "thrilling history" in the making.[80]

Such experiences were gradually winning converts to woman suffrage, particularly from the ranks of the more conservative who had viewed suffrage as a rather radical step. Throughout the last decade of the nineteenth century and into the early twentieth century, the Nineteenth Century Club membership moved closer to endorsement of woman suffrage. Not only were these club women beginning to feel comfortable about their involvement in legislative proceedings, but like those of the Woman's Christian Temperance Union, they recognized the need of full participation in the democratic process if they were going to succeed with prompt enactment of their reform ideas.

There were individual members who had long favored woman suffrage and had worked actively on its behalf,[81] but just as many of the women were opposed. When the Association for the Advancement of Women assembled at the Nineteenth Century Club in 1892 for its annual convention, a suffrage symposium was held at the request of many local women. However, significant opposition to suffrage was also expressed, and "consternation" from "a large element of club women not in sympathy with the suffrage movement" was noted.[82] Because women suffrage held great potential for divisiveness, the Nineteenth Century Club did not attempt to formulate any official position. The members who pursued an interest in suffrage did so through associations formed for that specific purpose.

As women's public involvement increased, support for woman suffrage grew. By 1910 it became common practice for the Equal Suffrage Association to hold its meetings — to which all Nineteenth Century Club members were routinely invited — at the Nineteenth Century Club.[83] In 1916, the year following the long campaign to win the Eligibility of Women on Boards bill, the Nineteenth Century Club advised its delegates to the convention of the Tennessee Federation of Women's Clubs to endorse the principle of equal suffrage. This was the first official expression of support for suffrage by the Nineteenth Century Club as a group. The executive board of the Nineteenth Century Club subsequently voted unanimously in 1918 to send a telegram to the chairman of the committee on the suffrage amendment in Washington on behalf of "the largest woman's club in the South," urging passage of the proposed amendment.[84] Furthermore, a number of Nineteenth Century Club members played leading roles in the struggle for ratification, the final battle taking place in the Tennessee legislature.[85] These actions left little doubt as to the sentiment of the Nineteenth Century Club about voting rights for women, but the early initiatives and leadership on this issue had originated elsewhere. In the case of woman suffrage, the reforming impulse had been brought to the Nineteenth Century Club, where it gradually and finally gained acceptance and support.

Annual announcements of the Nineteenth Century Club reveal the women's broad range of interest in educational issues, and club members became leading activists in the city's educational affairs — from the sponsorship of kindergartens to the establishment of a normal school. In 1888, two years before the founding of the Nineteenth Century Club, the Memphis Free Kindergarten was established by "a small band of noble women concerned about neglected children."[86] All of these women would later become members of the Nineteenth Century Club, which took over the sponsorship of the kindergarten association. The kindergarten idea was considered very experimental, but the women were convinced of its necessity in the educational development of children. Circumstances, they believed, should not be allowed to prevent any child from having the opportunity to receive the equipment necessary for the "battle of life," and this early preparation was thought an essential component in the production of "an industrious and skilled class of workers with honest pride and independence."[87] By 1892 the women felt the kindergarten idea had "taken root," and it was their sponsorship that ultimately resulted in legislation in 1913 providing for the establishment of kindergartens in public schools in Tennessee cities of five thousand or more people.[88]

The establishment of the West Tennessee State Normal School in Memphis also carried the imprint of the Nineteenth Century Club. From its earliest days, the club had counted educators among its membership; and in the campaign to have the normal school located in Memphis, the leadership provided by such women as Lillian Wyckoff Johnson and Elizabeth Messick was crucial. Both were professional educators who devoted much of their lives to the advocacy of higher education for southern women and their active participation in public life. Both were members of the Nineteenth Century Club.

Johnson, the daughter of Elizabeth Fisher and J. C. Johnson, was a "second generation" activist, carrying on the legacy of her mother's pioneering humanitarianism. The *Press Scimitar* described Lillian Johnson as a "pioneer. . . . She stepped out ahead of the crowd to meet the human needs she saw. Many followed the example she set. Others who did not were at least inspired by her courage, her selflessness, and her zest for living."[89]

Just as her mother had received an education unusual for a southern woman of that era, Lillian Johnson was also given such an opportunity and at age fifteen attended the recently opened Wellesley College. She received her B.A. degree from the University of Michigan in 1891 and returned to Memphis, where she joined the faculty of the Clara Conway Institute. The following year she became instructor of history at Vassar, where she remained for five years. Her studies then took her abroad to the Sorbonne and to Leipzig before returning to the United States to study at Cornell, where she received a Ph.D. degree in 1902 and became the first woman to hold the Andrew D. White Fellowship in medieval history.[90] Subsequently, she spent four years as president of Western College for Women in Oxford, Ohio, before returning to Memphis in 1907. Johnson was teaching at what became Central High School when in 1909 the Tennessee legislature passed a bill providing for the establishment of a normal school in each of the state's three grand divisions.[91] She was appointed by the Nineteenth Century Club as its official representative on the normal school issue and joined with Elizabeth Messick, County Superintendent of Public Instruction and vice-chairman of the Nineteenth Century Club's Education Department, in arousing Memphians to the importance of having the school situated in Memphis.[92]

The Education Department of the Nineteenth Century Club had been working for several years to stir interest in bringing higher education to the city, and in 1906 a committee had been formed to contact other organizations in an effort to enlist their cooperation.[93] A mass meeting had been held at the Nineteenth Century Club, attended by representatives from businesses, clubs, and educational associations. Bishop Thomas F. Gailor spoke on the "Urgent Need of a College in Memphis," and similar addresses were given by Mayor James Malone and Judge F. H. Heiskell. While interest grew, endowment funds were scarce. When the legislature acted to appropriate monies for normal schools, the Nineteenth Century Club decided to act swiftly. They had hoped for a university but shifted their focus and used the groundwork laid for higher education to promote teacher training. Johnson, Messick, and Mabel Williams — who succeeded Messick as city Superintendent of Public Schools — went to work mobilizing public support from men in the civic and business community and prompting press coverage. The Board of Education appointed a committee to concentrate solely on winning the school for Memphis, and Mayor Malone also appointed a general campaign committee of citizens. Of the twenty-one on the mayor's committee, seven were women, with Nineteenth Century Club members predominating.[94]

In June 1909, when news reports indicated that other cities in West Tennessee were making strong headway in their own campaign to win the school, Johnson and Williams again developed "spirited plans for quicker and increased action." They initiated a drive to raise private and public funds for the school as additional evidence of the good faith of the Memphis citizenry. Lillian Johnson directed women solicitors in Memphis, and Williams had charge of contributions outside the city. The women also appealed to the Legislative Council for concrete action, and in mid-June the *Memphis Commercial Appeal* congratulated the "public-spirited club women of Memphis" upon winning approval from the Legislative Council for a $100,000 bond issue for the erection of the state normal school. The newspaper commented: "If the ladies . . . held their heads unusually high last night, they were fully justified in so doing. . . . Their victories were won . . . through their persistent efforts in arousing public sentiment through many long months of work."[95]

The decision was made to locate the school for West Tennessee in Memphis, and on September 10, 1912, the West Tennessee State Normal School officially opened. Perhaps in recognition of the founding role played by the Nineteenth Century Club, its president, Mrs. James McCormack, delivered the first commencement address in 1913.[96]

Because of the Nineteenth Century Club's growing reputation as a significant force in molding public opinion, individuals and special interest groups increasingly turned to them for support. At a meeting of the Nineteenth Century Club in June 1910, for example, Henry Hanson of the Workingmen's Civic League, made an appeal for assistance in winning uniform laws for the protection of women and child laborers throughout the southern states. In urging them to support legislation and enforcement of existing labor laws, he pointed out the great influence club women had in creating public opinion.[97]

As early as 1902, the Nineteenth Century Club had shown interest in local labor issues, particularly as they affected the lives of women and children. Mrs. M. M. Betts, chairman of the Department of Philanthropy, and her committee sponsored a club program entitled "Industrial Conditions for Women and Children in Memphis." Various committee members reported on such things as "The Retail Shop," "The Pants Factories," "Box and Cracker Factories," and "Child Labor in Memphis."[98] They continued their programs the following year, indicating a positive response from the general membership, and sponsored a study on "Investigation of Conditions Surrounding Salesmen in Business Hours."[99] When Memphis telephone operators struck the Cumberland Telephone Company in 1907 for higher wages, Betts and Sarah Beaumont Kennedy led the Nineteenth Century Club in adopting a resolution supporting the female strikers.[100]

Throughout the first two decades of the twentieth century, the Nineteenth Century Club took public stands favoring workers and supported organizations dedicated to bettering employment conditions. Like the Woman's Christian Association before them, the Nineteenth Century Club also worked to provide "respectable housing" for young working women,[101] but they were much more vocal about the need for changed working conditions and government's responsibility for legislation to accomplish such changes.

In 1910 when the Textile and Child Labor Conference was held in Memphis, a special committee of the Nineteenth Century Club was formed to "assist the conference in any way possible," and the general membership held a reception honoring Florence Kelley and Jean Gordon, who had come to Memphis for the meeting.[102] They also formed a committee to interview candidates for public office on their positions concerning child and women workers, and the club became a dues-paying member of the Association for the Protection of Child and Women Labor in the Southern States.[103]

Locally the Nineteenth Century Club was identified as the organization that represented a helping hand for the working woman. The club received requests for help from wage-earning women and from other organizations, who asked for cooperation and support on a specific issue or, in some instances, to launch an investigation into a specific grievance. In 1910 Dr. Elizabeth Kane reported that the Nineteenth Century Club's Health Department, of which she

The Elizabeth Club. One of two boarding residences for young working women founded by the Girls' Welfare Committee of the Nineteenth Century Club. (Courtesy Mississippi Valley Collection.)

was chairman, was working on enforcement of the law requiring seats for women clerks in local department stores. The club, via its various committees, monitored working conditions in stores, calling attention to such things as sanitary conditions of bathrooms and the attitudes of floor managers toward female employees, and they petitioned the stores for earlier closing hours on Saturday nights.[104]

By 1920 the Nineteenth Century Club had carved for itself a solid position as a responsible force in civic reform and a group to be reckoned with in regard to the direction of city affairs. It had introduced the concept of the departmental woman's club to Memphis, and had successfully enlisted the support of a wide segment of women in projects of municipal improvement. The quality of life had been advanced, and because of the club's efforts and influence Memphis was becoming a more progressive and humanely directed city.

Nineteenth Century Club members were correctly perceived as women of elite standing who enjoyed, for the most part, relative financial security and leisure time. Their husbands tended to be professionals and businessmen — presidents of banks and cotton companies, judges, landowners, and high city officials. Such family connections allowed their wives immediate access to important power sources, as well as exempting them from much potential criticism. But the club was not a "closed society" of self-appointed provincial elites. While club women valued gentility and "standards" and were hardly revolutionaries, they were women who often were well-traveled, increasingly sophisticated, and informed about the work of activist women in other parts of the country.

Proselytizing had always been a Nineteenth Century Club practice and they attempted to interest as many women as possible in their work. The club attracted educated and enlightened women, a trend that continued through the years. When President Taylor of Vassar addressed the Nineteenth Century Club in 1905, there were eleven Vassar graduates in the audience, including Mattie Jones who had been president of the club in 1902.[105] Grace Carlile Smith and Augusta Lamar Heiskell were Wellesley graduates — Heiskell was president of the club in 1905 and Smith was a charter member.

The Nineteenth Century Club also attracted professional women, such as Clara Conway and Jenney Higbee among the early members, and Elizabeth Messick, Lillian Johnson, and Elizabeth Kane in the succeeding generation. While the number of professionals was small, it is significant that all of these women found their way to the Nineteenth Century Club. They saw the club as a forum through which real change in the city and in women's lives could be effected. By their presence and their work they enlarged traditional ways of thinking about how women should live their lives.

Collectively, the women of the Nineteenth Century Club possessed a finely honed sense of how far to step and in what directions they could maneuver without being perceived as a threat to the established order. Through their club work they had built a distinct public identity accompanied by a heightened sense of female self-worth. These southern women would no longer retreat into prayer and self-flagellation for wanting to exercise more control over life's events and, specifically, the direction of their own lives. They no longer lived lives of rural isolation but now had means of regular, productive, and creative contact with other women, which provided them with a strong support network. While innovation in women's lives was already underway in Memphis via the reformism of the Women's Christian Association and the Woman's Christian Temperance Union, the Nineteenth Century Club brought the women's club movement to Memphis full-fledged, greatly expanding opportunities and adding a certain amount of unity to female activism.

The Nineteenth Century Club members believed club life meant a freer life for women and hoped clubs would become an essential element in all women's lives. As Frances Cole, the retiring president in 1916, expressed it:

> Today comes to a close a year that has been to me the happiest and most helpful of any I have yet known. It has put into my life such tender friendships, and by a closer association I have learned a higher valuation of women. I am proud of our large and capable membership and I am so ambitious that we do not cease our efforts to interest women in joining until every woman in Memphis . . . has become a member.[106]

Membership reached a peak in 1926 when there were approximately 1,400 members. A Business Woman's Department had been added in 1920, and several years later a Junior Department for young women aged sixteen through twenty-seven. However, after 1929 membership declined, and the club referred to "the devastating effects of the recent depression years," after which their former numbers were never recovered.[107]

By broadening their appeal and attempting to attract as many women as possible, they may have become too diverse. The Nine-

The Nineteenth Century Club's location since 1926. (Courtesy of the Nineteenth Century Club.)

teenth Century Club had attempted to become all things to all women and in the process may have lost its focus. By the 1920s, a woman could enroll in everything from tap dancing to stenography to social service work; and, in light of the increasing educational opportunities for women, the "courses" offered by the Nineteenth Century Club no longer had the appeal they once did. Social reform, which had long been the Nineteenth Century Club's major identity, was becoming professionalized away from club women; and while social work remained a major category of interest to Nineteenth Century Club women, they increasingly became auxiliaries to established social service agencies. Such social functions as luncheons, teas, and balls increased, and the Nineteenth Century Club gradually disappeared from the cutting edge of social reform. As depression settled in after 1929, club dues may have seemed an unnecessary frill,[108] and — as often happens during periods of economic retrenchment — women retreated to the hearth.

While public activities through club work had expanded female roles, and woman's public presence had been well established, the next step—from public influence to public power—required fundamental change in the male-female hierarchy. This the Nineteenth Century Club had not altered, nor was it ever their intention to do so. The Nineteenth Century Club had been an enlightening influence in the lives of late nineteenth- and early twentieth-century Memphis women, but when the advancement of women again became a focal point of American society in the 1960s, the Nineteenth Century Club had long since lost its momentum as a catalyst for social change.

5

Suzanne Conlan Scruggs

While the Nineteenth Century Club provided entry for numerous women into public affairs, there was one whose activism was of such intensity and proportion as to warrant a separate account. This was Suzanne Conlan Scruggs, a Boston native who came to Memphis in 1889 following her marriage to Thomas M. Scruggs, a prominent attorney and later a judge. Heavily imbued with the progressive New England spirit, she found Memphis retrograde and unenlightened in the ways of civic development and lost little time associating herself with those committed to urban progress.[1] She became a founding member of the Nineteenth Century Club and served on its governing board.[2] Subsequently she became deeply committed to a vast number of civic and humanitarian enterprises, most of which were dedicated to the betterment of conditions for the city's children. Her membership in the Nineteenth Century Club provided a vital connection enabling her to draw upon an expanding network of women with clout and time to devote to philanthropic projects. While many of her reform ideas were carried out with the aid of Nineteenth Century Club members, the organizations formed for those purposes were entirely independent of the club, and Scruggs's public identity was that of a committed individual. Her personal activism and tireless pursuit of civic improvement were unparalleled in Memphis. Largely because of her initiatives, the playground movement was begun, a juvenile court established, and citizen involvement in public education developed and organized.

Her first public project was launched in 1894, when, in a meeting

of the governing board of the Nineteenth Century Club, she proposed a movement to raise the necessary funds to open the Cossit
Library, which stood finished but without books. There had been
a bequest from P. R. Bohlen of $2,400 for books, but it was con-
tingent upon a like amount being raised by citizens. Scruggs served
as chairman of the joint committee of the Nineteenth Century Club
and the Woman's Council to raise the necessary funds. Their efforts
were successful, and in 1894 the library was opened to the public.

Scruggs's civic work was interrupted by childbearing,[3] but it was
her children who refocused her attention on the city's shortcomings. As her offspring entered school, Scruggs became alarmed and
then outraged at what she described as "the deplorable condition
of public schools."[4] In early 1905, she launched an investigation of
the school system that led her and others into a chain of reforms
centering on the needs of the children of Memphis.

Scruggs believed that women bore the primary responsibility for
child rearing, a responsibility she interpreted in a very broad and
comprehensive sense, which amounted to her own version of municipal housekeeping. As children reached school age and went into
the community, she explained, it was a mother's "duty and obligation to broaden her interest which she can certainly do without
neglecting her home. It is the task of mothers to make safer conditions for the children of Memphis."[5] She described women as child
"experts" and urged their involvement in every aspect that touched
a child's development. Scruggs was genuinely convinced of woman's
"sphere." She temporarily gave up her membership in the Nineteenth
Century Club in the late 1890s and devoted herself entirely to home
duties. Upon seeing the status of the city's educational system, however, she became convinced that mothers would have to take up the
cause of reform. Citing an account in the *Boston Herald* of the Public School Association there, she began to publicize the need for
something similar in Memphis.[6]

Scruggs was energetic, thorough, well organized, and doggedly
determined—these characteristics marked all her efforts. She fully
immersed herself in the situation at hand, consulted organizations
and "experts" in other regions,[7] and enlisted the support of the local
press in publicizing her findings.[8] She could also be strident and

Suzanne Conlan Scruggs. A committed activist whose membership in the Nineteenth Century Club enabled her to draw upon an expanding network of women with clout and time to devote to civic improvement. Her initiatives included the establishment of the playground movement and the juvenile court system, and the development and organization of citizen involvement in public education. (Courtesy of Elizabeth L. Goodheart.)

overbearing in pursuit of her goals—which, when combined with an adversarial personality, sometimes lent a bitter tone to her efforts. Diplomacy was not her strong suit. In the discussions in 1905 surrounding the need for reform of the school system, she spoke of a "politically controlled school management," which she accused of "fraudulently" dealing with school funds and administering the system with "deplorable inefficiency" and very little regard for "the details of children's education."[9] These were indeed fighting words, and while she was successful in the formation of a public school association, it was not accomplished without a fight engendering a certain amount of bitterness. The relationship between the school board and the citizens' association was never a completely smooth one.

In launching the movement that led first to the formation of the Woman's Public School Association, Scruggs tapped the existing women's club network. She sent a report to a number of women's organizations in which she detailed the need for improvement of the city's schools and asked their cooperation in finding solutions.[10] She invited their participation in a meeting for the purpose of organizing a women's association to monitor the schools, explaining:

> The object of this meeting is to discuss the necessity of improvements in our public school system, and to formulate some practical suggestions as to how these improvements can be effected. In other cities the value of the counsel and co-operation of women in the management of the public schools has been recognized for many years by the election of women upon the school board.[11]

She pointed out that for almost three decades Boston had a female chairman of the school board, and, while Scruggs was not openly advocating woman's candidacy in Memphis, she contended that surely "It is not an unwarranted intrusion upon the province of those who manage our public schools, for an association of women to come together for the purpose of discussing the application of the present system to the needs of the children now in these schools."[12]

Nevertheless, "certain of these officials scorned suggestions from mere women," and while others knew about the "deplorable inefficiency" in the educational system, they resented women's interference with "personal prerogatives." Scruggs charged that school officials had grown used to running things with no oversight, and had come to regard the school system as "their legitimate province."[13]

At the ensuing meeting held at the rooms of the Housekeepers' Club, Scruggs spoke at length, propounding with great zeal her views on the crucial nature of public education and manifesting a genuine concern for all children regardless of their economic standing:

> As a public investment, none can be better than the schools, and as a public charge none should inspire more interest in the public mind; because upon the efficiency of these schools largely depends the harvest of good citizenship we will reap ten or a dozen years from now. The destinies of the children will be greatly influenced by our zeal and interest or by our indifference.[14]

Scruggs then presented her "Report on the Reorganization of the School System," which she had compiled from school board records. It was a meticulously prepared and scathing report documenting what she believed were the greatest shortcomings of the Memphis system. She pointed out that 97 percent of the students were too old for their grades. This she termed "retardation" and was due, she said, to an "unwise" and "poorly thought out system of examination and promotion." She called attention to "poverty in the curriculum," "unfit books," "unhygienic conditions," and overcrowding in some rooms while there was vacant space in others. She also noted the appalling dropout rate. Moreover, those few who did complete the high school course required one to two years further study to meet college entrance requirements. Her report was printed in the *Memphis Commercial Appeal* and subsequently distributed in pamphlet form.[15]

The school board's response was cool, but there was no immediate refutation of Scruggs's findings. In a meeting at the Nineteenth Century Club at which Scruggs had spoken on the need for school reform, the assistant superintendent of Memphis public schools, Wharton Jones,[16] stated that it would be futile to attempt the changes suggested by Mrs. Scruggs because of inadequate finances, and he refused to answer any questions.[17] No doubt Scruggs's findings were an embarrassment to administrators despite their aloof response.

Never hesitant about direct confrontation, Scruggs then went beyond charges of inefficiency. According to the terms of its charter, the school board was required to publish a full annual report including financial information, yet as of 1905, she claimed, there had been no report for six years. Scruggs directly questioned the honesty of officials and demanded a full public accounting. She suggested that the political ambitions of some public officials had been put above the needs of the school children, and behind such inefficiency lay "political intrigue" and possibly "graft," and "to keep silent on such matters" would make one "as guilty as the public school officials."[18] Such direct accusations proved unsettling to some of her cohorts in the Nineteenth Century Club, and they attempted to sidetrack Scruggs's plan for a watchdog citizens' group to monitor the schools. In June 1905, at the meeting called for the purpose of forming the public school association, they attempted to put obstacles in the way of its formation by setting high dues to discourage membership and by insisting that members of the Board of Education should be invited to join. These tactics only stiffened Scruggs's resolve, and she accused the "antis" of sacrificing "honor to self-interest."[19] Scruggs contended that their actions were motivated by concern for the political ambitions of their husbands, who were connected to the school or city administration.[20] Nevertheless, the Woman's Public School Association was organized at the meeting in the form Scruggs had suggested, with their motto being "To the Public Good Private Respects Must Yield." The private respects did not yield gracefully, however, and a certain amount of ill feeling remained.

Scruggs forfeited her membership in the Nineteenth Century Club in 1908 over some differences regarding dues, which may well have been related to personal enmities begun by the school controversy.[21] Nonetheless, there was a close working relationship between the Woman's Public School Association and the Nineteenth Century Club, and there was much interchange of membership. The first president, vice-president, and secretary were all members of the Nineteenth Century Club, and of the eleven committees of the Woman's Public School Association, ten were headed by women who were members of the Nineteenth Century Club.[22]

Scruggs declined the presidency of the Woman's Public School Association, explaining that as she had already appeared before

the Board of Education and had been unsuccessful in winning implementation of her suggestions, a group of officers that did not
include her might be more effective. She did agree to chair the Committee on Reorganization of the School System in Primary and
Grammar Grades, feeling this was an area of strength and success
for her.[23]

Scruggs was a fervid democrat with an abiding faith in the power
and judgment of an awakened public interest. Her instincts convinced her that if informed, the people would invariably "do right."
Such beliefs underlay all her efforts and were an important key in
her reform activities. An educated public was a prerequisite for progress, she felt, since far too many decisions in government were
made in "dark chambers." She worked for maximum press exposure as a means of focusing public attention, because she was convinced that "the enlightenment, zeal and honesty of a community,
in matters either civic, state or national, are the direct reflection of
the enlightenment, zeal and honesty of the press. It is the press that
creates public demand which in turn is the measure of civic progress."[24] Particularly for those with no money and no privilege, the
press seemed their only avenue of expression: "Help the people —
the great army of working people — those who own neither carriages
nor automobiles — whose homes have not spacious lawns and veran-
das — who seldom take summer trips — yet who are the 'backbone'
of Memphis prosperity — help them to make known their needs and
desires, and to secure recognition,"[25] said Scruggs. These were the
people upon whom much of the future depended, Scruggs believed.
They were an essential ingredient in the city's growth, and the degree to which they were educated and informed would determine
the level of their subsequent participation in, and contribution to,
the life of the city.[26]

Scruggs's report on the schools had stirred interest in a number
of quarters, touching tender nerves in some places, and eliciting
appreciation from others. Its major tangible result, the Woman's
Public School Association, proved to be a thorn in the side of the
Board of Education, as the women relentlessly identified problems,
publicized them widely, and offered solutions that were received
with varying degrees of enthusiasm by administration officials.[27]

Much of the work undertaken by the Woman's Public School Association derived from Scruggs's original report. Although she did not assume official leadership until she became president in 1910, Scruggs's ideas were the driving force behind the association, and her influence was pervasive.

In 1905 the Woman's Public School Association began its work by petitioning the Board of Education for permission to interview teachers and principals about the school system and to allow inspection of school board records. The women assured the board that helpfulness, not interference, was the purpose. The goal of the Woman's Public School Association, they stressed, was solely that of "bettering the condition of the Memphis schools," and they had only "the best interests of the children . . . at heart."[28] Such assurances must have been of little comfort when the women began publicizing their findings. Guided largely by concerns expressed by Scruggs, they called attention to the large number of children too old for their grades. They pointed out the small number of high school graduates — particularly boys — and criticized what they considered a very flawed system of promotion which encouraged dropouts.[29] The women revealed that only 28 percent of the city's school-age population was enrolled in the public schools.[30] While press reports carried news of enrollment growth, Scruggs pointed out that the increase in the number of students was simply the result of growing population. The telling statistic, she said, was that the percentage increase in attendance was only half as much as the percentage increase in the school-age population. Scruggs compiled figures showing a decline between 1900 and 1908 in the percentages of average daily attendance vis à vis the scholastic population.[31] Memphis children were losing ground, she said, yet costs somehow continued to increase.

The high failure rate and dropouts were troubling indicators to Scruggs from the beginning of her school investigation — concerns she passed on to the Woman's Public School Association. Scruggs and Mrs. R. C. Newsum — who would become an officer in the Woman's Public School Association — had appeared before the Board of Education in April 1905, to discuss the problem of dropouts and failures (who were called "laggards), but to little avail. Their session with the Board of Education was described as a lengthy one — "not altogether a pleasant one" — and "there were several rather spirited passages between Scruggs and [Superintendent] General Gordon." Scruggs had also crossed swords with Assistant Superintendent Wharton Jones, and her suggestions for a more equitable grade-recording system, the hiring of additional teachers to deal with deficiencies, and the institution of summer school to help "laggards," appeared to be brushed aside.[32]

Yet shortly after the formation of the Woman's Public School Association changes began to be made. Perhaps because more publicity was focused upon these areas and the changes were backed by the Woman's Public School Association, the board recognized the need to listen and respond. In September 1905, the systems of grade recording and promotion were changed,[33] and the curriculum was overhauled to allow a choice of a general course, a commercial course, or a university-preparatory course.[34] Summer schools were also eventually instituted to help students make up deficiencies.[35] When Superintendent Gordon presented his report on the status of the schools in July 1905, one month after the formation of the Woman's Public School Association, he included a paragraph on "Search for New Ideas," in which he stated that both he and his assistant superintendent would be visiting at least three other cities annually for the purpose of finding new ideas and methods for improving the schools.[36] The Board of Education often listened to the women grudgingly, but time and time again carried out their suggestions for change, even though the source was not always acknowledged openly or gratefully.

However, there were some changes instigated by the Woman's Public School Association that were carried out in cooperation with the Board of Education. The women urged the inclusion of manual training in the curriculum and presented "voluminous exhibits" illustrating courses of study used successfully in other cities. The board was quite receptive and answered that manual training had long been their wish as well.[37] Implementation just a few months after the Woman's Public School Association focused attention upon the idea suggests their prodding may well have provided the necessary impetus.

Some other cooperative ventures involved the identification and removal of obstacles to school attendance — a priority of the Woman's Public School Association. The cost of transportation and expense of books and supplies were targeted as factors that kept many children from poor families away from school. The women petitioned the Memphis Street Railway Company, with the endorsement of the Board of Education, and won half-fares for school children during school hours.[38] They also organized a book exchange through the Cossitt Library, whereby students could bring discarded books which were then given to needy children at no charge or at a very small one. The women eventually made strides toward convincing the Board of Education of the need for free books and supplies, and while school officials begged off by citing heavy indebtedness, they acknowledged the school system's responsibility.

Another obstacle to attendance attacked by the women was the issue of children's health, and in this area they met considerable resistance. The Woman's Public School Association believed that a regular system of medical inspection of children would prevent the spread of contagious diseases, as well as provide a means by which good health and hygiene could be promoted. The indefatigable Scruggs led the way, and in the fall of 1906 sent a letter to some one hundred physicians, health and school officials, and educators in Memphis and throughout the United States, asking their opinion of the desirability of medical inspection in the schools. Her investigation revealed that many cities in the Northeast already had such a program, but it was nonexistent in the South. The information was forwarded to the Board of Education, but no action was taken. In her capacity as chair of the Department of Education of the Nineteenth Century Club, and chair of the Committee on Physical Welfare of School Children of the Woman's Public School Association, Scruggs initiated a meeting held on November 22, 1906, at which prominent physicians and business leaders were invited to give their views on the medical-inspection idea.[39] The group was very enthusiastic, and speeches and comments made at the meeting were published in pamphlets and distributed throughout the city — a strategy used by Scruggs when she led in the formation of the Woman's Public School Association. It was also agreed that a permanent organization to deal with issues bearing on the schools would be beneficial, and at this meeting the Public Education Association was formed. Dr. R. B. Maury, a retired physician, served as president, with a number of prominent men included as officers. Scruggs served as corresponding secretary and Elizabeth Messick as a vice-president.[40]

The women recognized the need for additional influence, which the formation of the Public Education Association provided. They believed male cooperation would contribute the civic clout necessary to achieve controversial goals. As was the case with the House-keepers' Club, it was again the women's initiative that brought prominent men into reform, which the women felt would work for the benefit of all.

In a meeting of the school board in August 1907, the matter of medical inspection was discussed and reservations expressed concerning who would perform the inspections and how extensive they would be. Some felt medical inspections were unnecessary in a city such as Memphis. Dr. E. A. Neely, president of the Board of Education, announced that the matter had been considered but rejected as impracticable. In very large cities with foreign tenement-house populations, where people lived "amid the most unsanitary conditions," regular medical inspection would be justified. But, explained Neely, Memphis was not such a place, and the board was against a physical examination of such a broad scope.[41]

Yet the women finally won their point. The president of the Board of Health was persuaded to introduce an ordinance to the city council providing for regular medical inspections of children in the public schools, and by September 1908, free examinations at the city dispensary were being carried out. All children were required to be vaccinated and have a certificate before entering school.[42] The Board of Health also began making regular inspections of the schools in order to monitor sanitary conditions.

Two other projects spearheaded by Scruggs, which grew directly out of her involvement in the Public Education Association, were the playground movement and the establishment of the juvenile court. Juvenile delinquency had become a serious problem accompanying the growth of urbanization. Nationwide in the late nineteenth century, the playground and juvenile court movements occurred simultaneously as complimentary parts of "childsaving" efforts. Scruggs was very much aware of the increased focus placed upon the physical and moral development of the country's youth. She had corresponded with officials of several national organizations dedicated to bettering the lot of children, and she became determined to introduce those ideas to Memphis.

Scruggs's attention turned first to organizing constructive recreational facilities; and, almost immediately following the formation of the Public Education Association in 1906, she formed a playground committee as an arm of that association and became its chairman. She launched a public opinion blitz to garner citizen support for the idea, which began with the publication of a pamphlet entitled "For A Better Memphis." Relying heavily upon those whom she considered "experts," the pamphlet reflected the influence of the Playground Association of America, Judge Ben B. Lindsey — the acknowledged founder of the juvenile court movement in America — and Joseph Lee, president of the Massachusetts Civic League. Quoting Lee, Scruggs urged Memphians to recognize that "the most valuable asset of a city is its children." If their development is ignored, she warned, "many of these could become a liability."[43]

The care and development of children, Scruggs explained, had become a science, and intelligent, informed citizens should be aware of modern methods and put them to use. She chided Memphis for being far behind other cities and argued that to be "up to date" a city had to provide playgrounds — meaning "a properly equipped and supervised area within walking distance of every child in the city."[44] Scruggs pointed out that 336 cities in the United States had public playgrounds, and 300 of these were smaller and less important than Memphis. A city of "undoubted material prosperity," Memphis was doing little for the welfare of her children. The recently formed "Boosting Committee" which was about to spend fifty thousand dollars advertising the advantages Memphis offered to workers and families would do well, she said, to address themselves to "the need for quality of life," especially since so much emphasis was being put on making the city bigger.[45]

Scruggs sent articles and reports to the press detailing the needs of children and pointing out the beneficial impact playgrounds would have upon the city. She stressed that playgrounds were not a charity. They were regarded nationally as a civic institution just like schools — in fact, they were schools in the broadest sense, she explained. Playgrounds and recreation centers could provide an opportunity for many "unfortunate" and "forgotten" children to develop into useful and credible manhood and womanhood. She pointed out that playgrounds had been shown to save court costs and jail expenditures — more than would be sufficient to maintain playgrounds.[46] Paraphrasing Jane Addams, Scruggs said, "The great majority of the crimes that make jails necessary owe their origin in youth to a misdirected craving for recreation. . . . the play impulse gone awry. Better a playground spot than a court and a jail when the harm is done."[47]

Another step in her campaign to win support for playgrounds was to bring the field secretary of the Playground Association of America, Lee Hanmer, to Memphis. Hanmer delivered an address outlining the beneficial impact playgrounds were having across the country and advised Memphis on how to proceed in establishing a system.[48] Scruggs carefully orchestrated Hanmer's visit. She wrote personal letters to numerous businessmen, clerics, educators, and public officials, urging them to attend Hanmer's lecture and asking for their support for a local movement. One businessman, Mr. P. P. Van Vleet, replied that while he would be out of the city, he was "heartily in favor" of such work and encouraged her to call on him for assistance.[49] Another, Robert Galloway, who since his retirement from business had been serving as chairman of the Park Commission, replied that for a couple of years he had been interested in introducing playground features into the Memphis parks and suggested a meeting to decide which grounds could best be used to begin these projects.[50]

Adept at organizing public opinion, Scruggs had succeeded in creating a groundswell of positive support. The Memphis Playground Association was formed in the spring of 1908 and a charter from the state secured in August.[51] Representatives from the Cotton Exchange, the Businessmen's Club, the Builders Exchange, and Federation of Women's Clubs, had all cooperated in its establishment, and several leading citizens were numbered among its incorporators.[52]

In 1908 the Park Commission agreed to equip a playground at Brinkley Park. Financial maintenance was provided by a committee of doctors and lawyers who raised the money through benefit baseball games. The proceeds provided supervisors, an athletic director, and a female director to teach the younger children sewing and singing. By the spring of 1909, the Park Commission had appropriated $450 for equipment for three more parks—Overton, Gaston, and Bickford. Indeed, noted Scruggs, such progress was encouraging but much remained to be done. The doctors' and lawyers' committee did not sustain their commitment, and supervision had to be dropped at Brinkley Park. A few unsupervised play spaces with playground apparatus, Scruggs pointed out, hardly fulfilled the nationally accepted idea of a playground system, any more than a few buildings equipped with desks and blackboards fulfilled the idea of a public school system. There was as great a need for constant supervision of playgrounds as there was for teachers she argued, and in 1910 she began working for commitment from the city to provide paid supervisors. Scruggs believed there was much support among the citizenry for a comprehensive plan for playgrounds in Memphis, but the problem lay in convincing the municipal bureaucracy to commit funds. As Scruggs pointed out, "The park board is waiting for the school board and the school board is waiting for the commissioner. Each is sure the task belongs to the other department."[53]

Funding remained a problem for the Playground Association as their requests for money were shifted from one government department to another. However, in 1914 the Department of Recreation was created with a budget of twelve thousand dollars for the first year's work.[54] The Recreation Commission absorbed the Playground Association and by 1915 was acknowledged "as a definite part of city government." The educational value of play was said to be recognized "as an important factor in the development of child life."[55] Trained directors were on the grounds at six parks, and play hours had been established at the Church Home, Leath Orphan Asylum, juvenile court, and Fresh Air Home. The press observed that "It should be a source of pride to the citizens of Memphis to know that this city is well advanced in this phase of social work, and a visit to any one of the playgrounds would be a pleasure as well as an education in what is being done in this field."[56]

Scruggs was also the key figure in the establishment of a juvenile court in Memphis, which developed side by side with the Playground Association. One of her initial acts as president of the Memphis Playground Association was the appointment of a juvenile court committee to lay the groundwork for such a court in Memphis. Samuel O. Bates, subsequently elected to the state legislature, served as chairman of the committee which included Wassell Randolph, a local attorney; W. L. Terry, a banker; Marion Griffin, Tennessee's first female lawyer; and Scruggs herself. Via a network of well-placed friends and business associates, they began to mobilize public opinion.

The housing of children with older criminals was common practice throughout the country. In 1901 the Colorado law, inspired by Judge Ben Lindsey, which created a juvenile court and provided for separation of juveniles and adults, became a model for reformers. Scruggs was quite familiar with the work of Judge Lindsey. She had corresponded with him about juvenile delinquency and was greatly influenced by his ideas, which she publicized in Memphis.[57] There had also been some concern in Memphis because of juvenile crime prior to the formation of Scruggs's committee, so efforts to win backing for the establishment of a juvenile court did not begin from ground zero.

In 1904 a reformatory for boys had been opened with enthusiastic citizen support, including crucial fund-raising efforts led by the women of the Friends of the Needy Circle of the King's Daughters.[58] The congregation of the Chelsea Presbyterian Church had organized its own "Juvenile Protective Association" in 1907 to befriend children in trouble.[59] The awareness of the city's need for an institution of broader scope and permanence to deal with the problem of youth crime was growing, and the formation of the Playground Association in 1908 helped crystalize opinion in favor of action. Thus the Memphis public was quite receptive to the idea of a juvenile court. In 1909 Samuel Bates and the Shelby County delegation introduced the bill to establish a juvenile court in Memphis. That bill, originally drawn up by Marion Griffin and worked into final form by Wassell Randolph, embodied the philosophy and advice of Judge Lindsey. However, as the bill made its way through the legislature, it was amended, making the new court a criminal court with policemen serving as probation officers. The Scruggs contingent was very unhappy with the amended bill and charged it was "a direct violation of the fundamental principle of the Juvenile Court"[60] and that "political influence" had "conspired" to change the original bill.[61] After much heated discussion, Scruggs and her supporters, guided by the strategy that "half a loaf is better than none," supported the bill, and on April 27, 1909, the Bates bill became law.[62]

Scruggs remained dissatisfied because the juvenile court was under the authority of the police department, and she continued to make public criticisms charging that "intolerable wrongs" were being committed upon helpless children."[63] In a letter to Governor Ben Hooper, Scruggs wrote that she had ample proof that "the most appalling moral wrongs to little girls is carried on not only with the knowledge, but actually under the protection of the Police Department." As a branch of the city police court, the juvenile court was "dominated by the same corrupt influences," and she chided Mayor Crump for his seeming unwillingness to recognize the situation and put a stop to it.[64] She continued to insist that

> All Juvenile Court authorities are emphatic in declaring that the Juvenile Court should have no connection whatever with Police or Criminal Courts, and that probation officers should not be selected from the police department. Judge Lindsey emphasizes that a Juvenile Court should be a court not of criminal jurisdiction alone (as a Police Court) but a Court having all the criminal, chancery and civil jurisdiction necessary to cases pertaining to children, parents or others affected by the juvenile laws.[65]

Feeling very strongly that the juvenile court was not addressing many problems related to delinquency, Scruggs organized the Children's Protective Union. As that organization's president, she described its function as "supplemental" to the juvenile court[66] and recruited organizations involved in "childhelping work" as members. The member groups represented a wide segment of citizens,[67] and the union was accepted by municipal authorities as an unofficial arm of the juvenile court. Provided with an office in the court house, the Children's Protective Union performed auxiliary functions for which the court lacked the necessary manpower and organizational apparatus. They focused particularly upon children who were neglected and often homeless, receiving cases from the court as well as referrals from individuals. Through their Children's Aid Committee, which became known as the Friendly Visitor, volunteers visited homes, evaluated needs, and attempted to provide means to relieve problems found there.

Much of their work dealt with finding homes for children. "There has been a great need in Memphis of a bureau through which this home finding could be regularly conducted,"[68] Scruggs explained, and she herself held countless interviews with prospective adoptive parents, meticulously checking the moral and financial standing of applicants.[69] She pointed out that the orphanages of the city were overcrowded, which had necessitated turning away homeless children; but that even before such overcrowding, their policies had excluded many children, since boys over nine and girls over twelve were not eligible for admission. The "capacity of each of these worthy institutions is taxed to its utmost to care for children below these ages," Scruggs said, which had forced them to adopt age limits.[70] While the Home of the Good Shepherd existed for wayward girls, and the Shelby County Industrial School for boys, there was, she believed, a desperate need to help children over these ages who, while homeless, were not delinquent. Scruggs admonished: "The utter inadequacy of charitable provision for children's needs stands out more clearly each day. . . . No other city in the country ignores its responsibility to provide homes for dependent children of this tender age."[71]

The Children's Protective Union also tried to help families through times of difficulty, calling upon the varied resources provided by member organizations. They helped in locating jobs, arranged for medical attention or hospital treatment, and encouraged school attendance, hoping to "keep families together" and "preserve the home." As was the case with the Women's Christian Association, the Children's Protective Union prided itself on helping individuals and families to help themselves, believing that "mere alms-giving nearly always makes matters worse."[72]

A legislative committee was also formed to work for the enactment and enforcement of laws for child welfare, although in this area the women seemed to defer to the men. As they looked toward the new year of 1911, one goal was said to be "the leadership of a strong man as president, able to guide our efforts for necessary legislation." The "charity side" was deemed "more essentially" women's work.[73]

The idea of bringing in a man to spearhead the legislative program of the Children's Protective Union seems to have been Scruggs's strategy for winning increased male support in the work of reform for children. The "strength" of men was said to be needed in the "public world" of the legislature. Never mind that Scruggs herself worked as chair of the Legislative Committee of the Tennessee Congress of Mothers, and personified the adjective *strong*, she recognized the advantage of male influence — particularly with all-male legislatures. It was Scruggs who had encouraged men to become involved with school reform and engineered the formation of the Public Education Association. And it was Scruggs who had enlisted male support in creating the Playground Association and juvenile court. While women's ideas and initiative had guided the formation of these groups, male participation had added an important dimension.

While many women who were active in social reform soon adopted female suffrage as a necessary component, believing that only by changing the gender ratio in government would they achieve enactment of their ideas, Scruggs did not warm to suffrage until well into the twentieth century. While she had been critical of male dominance of education via the all-male Board of Education, and was a genuine and sincere proponent of an expanded sphere for women in areas that involved women and children, she believed the most direct route for bringing change to the lives of women and children was for women to throw all their energies into broadening "the reach of motherhood." She took the position that if women would involve themselves in community work, "wrong conditions" could be eliminated without suffrage.[74] By attracting an adequate number of powerful men to their causes, legislatures could be won over, she believed.

Scruggs had no philosophical quarrel with women in public or political life, as her own life affirms. Her comments in 1914, when reporting on the care of delinquent girls, certainly reveal sentiments favorable to woman suffrage: "So many girls' souls have been bartered and bodies defiled by the crimes of men who wield the power of the ballot that is denied women. The men who are responsible for the degradation of these pitiful young girls elect the officials who control the machinery of our courts and our legislatures."[75] Yet, when the suffrage struggle reached a peak in Tennessee with the battle for ratification of the nineteenth amendment, Scruggs was not among the activists. She was more inclined to channel her efforts into reforms that she believed had more immediate impact upon women's and children's welfare, and suffrage, she felt, did not fit the category.

While heavily committed to projects connected to the Children's Protective Union, Scruggs's involvement in school reform never lessened. Her work in this area broadened considerably when in January 1911, a Tennessee branch of the National Congress of Mothers was formed and Scruggs became vice-president for West Tennessee.[76] Through statewide networks they hoped to organize support on matters relating to child welfare — one objective being the promotion of closer relations between schools and home. Parent-Teacher Associations were formed, and in Memphis there was one for each school district, with a central union of which the ubiquitous Scruggs became president. She commented that until Tennessee gave women a voice in the conduct of the schools, the most effective way to make their influence felt was via Parent-Teacher Associations, which provided a means to study problems that concerned child welfare at home, at school, and in the community.[77] The Parent-Teacher Association was very active, bringing many women into projects for the schools, and focusing public attention on issues relating to women and children. In 1914 the Memphis Parent-Teacher Association launched a campaign for child welfare and inaugurated bimonthly meetings open to the public to discuss such matters as vocational training, recreation, child labor, widows' pensions, hygiene, the school as a social center, and juvenile delinquency.[78] It was largely through the efforts of the Parent-Teacher Association that a vocational high school was opened, an infant milk depot established, and a better-babies movement launched.

It was also during these years that school finances moved to center stage. A controversy erupted in 1911 when the Board of Education requested a $250,000 bond issue. Scruggs, long dissatisfied with the board's annual reports, led the attack, which focused on the financial accounting methods of the school administration. Scruggs appeared before the city commissioners and launched a "sensational attack," which excoriated the Board of Education for failure to provide proper accounting for previous bond issues.[79] She charged that the last bond issue of $500,000, in 1909, had not yet been accounted for, that the reports were "fragmentary," that "false statements" had been made, and she argued that any new funds should be delayed until a full accounting for past expenditures was provided. Then, said Scruggs, "Let the people pass upon the merits of the claim before the city commission."[80] A number of women's clubs formed special ad hoc committees to discuss the situation. The press lined up behind Scruggs, saying her request for a full public accounting from the board was "not only reasonable but required by the charter which created the board. . . . What kind of Memphis public have we anyway, that will stand back and let a woman — singlehanded — fight their battles for them? . . . Wake up, Mr. Taxpayer!"[81]

Mayor Crump, who had cautioned Scruggs against making such serious accusations[82] and had declared himself satisfied by the Board of Education's accounting, felt the need to appoint a special committee to investigate the charges of financial ineptitude.[83] Scruggs requested a public hearing before the Mayor's special committee to discuss the needs of school children. She said a number of mothers as well as a number of teachers and principals would like to give their views. "This great teaching force is better qualified to judge as to school needs than the men who by the accident of political preference are members of the school board."[84] Scruggs made it clear that she was not against money for education, but she felt more oversight of the Board of Education was needed. Her request for a hearing was not granted, and the mayor's special committee reported in favor of the bond issue, prompting the press to comment: "All they did was to say the money was needed — something already known. They failed to question the need for improvement in the schools or . . . the efficiency of the present school board or whether past funds had been properly spent. All they did was to report a need which had never been questioned."[85]

The school deficit reached a high of $210,000 by 1913, prompting the school administration to request a tax increase. Scruggs, in her capacity as chair of the Central Union of Parent-Teacher Associations, and vice-president of the West Tennessee Congress of Mothers, continued to berate the school board for failing to follow proper business practices. She insisted there should be no tax increase until the financial situation was remedied; and she presented a list of proposals for consideration, which included better salaries for teachers, kindergartens in every school district, equipment for industrial training in every school, and playgrounds in every school district.[86]

The deficit continued to grow, leading the Board of Education to discuss cuts in teachers' salaries just when Scruggs and the Parent-Teacher Association were requesting increases. The explosion came in 1914. The spark that ignited the furor was the school board's firing of two respected teachers, Cora Ashe and Mamie Cain, who had worked in the school system for many years. Wide support from men and women in the community coalesced around Ashe and Cain, and their reinstatement was demanded. At a school board meeting attended by an estimated 150 citizens, which was described as "beginning hysterically and disorderly," it was charged that the firings were retaliation against the teachers because they had opposed Mayor Crump's candidates in the last school board election.[87] J. P. Norfleet, chairman of the Board of Education, claimed that the board was acting in the best interests of the system and stated that the action against Ashe and Cain would not be rescinded. This brought "hisses from the women — club and society women, church workers and school teachers." One lady in the crowd remarked, "What a miserable board."[88]

Reminiscent of the "school board battle" in 1872 to 1873, this one, too, failed in its immediate goal of reinstating the fired teachers. But the long range impact was very important. Female represen-

Cora Henry Ashe. Cora Henry Ashe and Mamie Cain were two teachers at the center of a school controversy in 1914 which led to legislation making women eligible for election to the school board. Reproduced from *Woman's Work in Tennessee* (Memphis: Printed under the auspices of the Tennessee Federation of Women's Clubs by Jones Briggs Co., 1916).

Mamie Cain (Mrs. Joseph D. Browne). The firing of respected teachers Cora Ashe and Mamie Cain brought "hisses from the women — club and society women, church workers and school teachers." Reproduced from *Woman's Work in Tennessee* (Memphis: Printed under the auspices of the Tennessee Federation of Women's Clubs by Jones-Briggs Co., 1916).

tation on the school board was finally recognized as a crucial need, and broad-based community support developed behind the movement to make women eligible. In 1915 the Tennessee legislature enacted a bill accomplishing that goal, and the Tennessee Federation of Parent-Teacher Associations began organizing support behind a female candidate for the 1916 school board election.[89] Two women, Mrs. Walter Gray and Mrs. Isaac Reese, won seats on the Board of Education, providing Memphis teachers with a sympathetic ear. In 1917 when the Teachers' Association threatened a strike unless their salaries were increased, and one male board member suggested protestors should be dropped from the payroll, the women members came to the teachers' defense. Mrs. Reese pointed out that Memphis teachers had not been given a raise for ten years, and she declared herself to be in sympathy with their demands. While a strike did occur, no strikers lost their jobs, and a $10 per month increase was granted.

By winning representation on the Board of Education, the women had become a strong influence. From policy making at the top level, to the Parent-Teacher Association at the grass-roots level, women had become active agents in shaping the direction of the school system in Memphis; and Suzanne Scruggs had played a key role in initiating these changes.

Scruggs's years of involvement in community projects were characterized by intense activity. Arriving in a fledgling southern town in the late nineteenth century she found herself in a situation of urban backwardnesss, part of a female population whose attitude toward civic responsibility was at best unformed and at worst reluctant and irresolute. While feisty and too often abrasive for southern temperaments, she won the admiration of many, and she certainly energized the Memphis women's club scene. Injustice seemed to offend her inherent sense of equity, which may have been a legacy of her New England upbringing, and she was never reluctant to involve herself in causes she considered just.

Scruggs encouraged women to secure their assigned sphere firmly and forcefully; and, while many followed her lead, she was never loathe to act alone. In her sometimes single-handed pursuit of goals, she differentiated herself from other women-reformers in Mem-

Mrs. Isaac Reese. Mrs. Issac Reese served as president of the Nineteenth Century Club and the Memphis Woman's Club. In 1916, she
was one of the first of two women to be elected to seats on the Board
of Education. Reproduced from *Woman's Work in Tennessee* (Memphis: Printed under the auspices of the Tennessee Federation of
Women's Clubs by Jones Briggs Co., 1916).

phis, who tended to work more with associates and with a greater sense of connection to other women. While Scruggs was alert and sensitive to the southern male-female balance of power, she could be impatient with the structural constraints imposed by circumstances and culture. While secure in the elite culture of the city, Scruggs seemed removed from the heart of the women's network and remained somewhat of an outsider. Her disappearance from the reform scene after about 1917 is difficult to explain but may well have been the result of weariness from constant, and too often lonely, combat. She was tireless in her pursuit of right, and — once committed — she was a fighter who never backed off. Nonetheless, even Scruggs's relentless determination may have reached its limits.[90] During her active years, she had provided Memphis with significant leadership, and her efforts transformed the city in many ways.

Conclusion

In the late nineteenth and early twentieth centuries there were two important, closely interrelated directions being charted by elite, white women of Memphis. One was the creation of a public record and presence. The other was the formation of an autonomous realm — a woman's identity beyond family, from which a specifically female perspective was developed and applied to the larger world. In the process, the delicate male-female balance subtly shifted, as women took steps to address the restrictiveness which had for so long governed their lives under the antebellum patriarchy and under which they had long chafed. The history of the antebellum South is replete with evidence of women's discontent, but generations of subordination do not vanish overnight.

Generally speaking, women emerged from the Civil War carrying within themselves the seeds of a new self-definition. Their many cooperative efforts during the war contributed immeasurably to a developing sense of sisterhood and brought forth wide recognition of characteristics of strength and tenacity. The controversy surrounding the wage cut of female schoolteachers in Memphis in 1872 to 1873 registered the impact of changed economic conditions on women's attitudes, as well as evincing a collective sensitivity to women's subordination and a willingness to publicly express their discontent. No longer content to sit quietly and docilely in the face of injustices done to women, they were becoming a potent force. In the heat of debate, the women disputed openly and publicly the doctrine of female inferiority and made it clear that areas that concerned the management of children were their "natural" responsibility. It would be as the defenders of the family that women would claim for themselves a greater responsibility in the public world.

Increment by increment, the building blocks of an expanded female sphere were assembled. A confluence of social and economic factors created an atmosphere conducive to change in the patterns of women's lives, and they began to challenge male preemption of the public realm. As the city grew and prospered, the relative leisure and financial security of a growing number of women allowed participation in voluntary organizations. Increased urbanization facilitated communication locally, as well as heightening women's awareness of activities in other parts of the country. Improved educational access and the pervasive influence of evangelical religious tenets — impressing upon them the duty to create God's kingdom on earth — infused women with aspirations beyond home and family.

The Women's Christian Association, which drew its organizational strength from the female population of Memphis churches, was the first women's organization to focus exclusively upon the needs of women. While their insight into the problems of urban poverty was not incisive, their activities and projects heightened women's sense of personal and civic responsibility for the future development of the city — particularly where women and children were concerned. In gaining exposure to the difficulties faced by the poor, women developed a greater consciousness of their lack of control over the circumstances of their lives and the social, economic, and legal disabilities under which all women struggled. They searched and probed for ways and means by which women could improve their lives. They directed their efforts toward stamping out the evils of alcohol, dirt, filth and disease, hopelessness, delinquency, and a whole variety of urban ills. As the Women's Christian Association, the Woman's Christian Temperance Union, and the women's club movement addressed themselves to solutions to these problems, opportunities for female activism became almost limitless. The women succeeded in carving out for themselves a domain that historians have named municipal housekeeping, and upon this justification they built their new identity in the public arena.

Women had experienced success in running numerous charitable institutions, they had raised sizable sums of money in the community, and handled their own financial affairs with competence. They had dealt regularly with various government departments, in some cases being responsible for their inauguration. The city council, the mayor's office, the school board, the health department, and legislative halls were no longer strangers to women. They focused the attention of the public upon the crucial nature of quality of life and addressed themselves to bringing about change in the attitude and responsibility of government towards its citizens. Women won for themselves an imposing public visibility and changed the face of the city in some important ways.

However, public entry did not proceed in an unbroken line, neatly traceable from the 1870s through the early twentieth century. In Memphis there remained a great deal of hesitation on the part of women about injecting themselves into public issues. It was fairly common, for example, for a man to read the reports at the Women's Christian Association meetings, and Elizabeth Johnson lamented that too many women allowed the strictures of Saint Paul to deter them. They were careful to tailor their rhetoric so as not to offend males, making constant reassurances that women were not "usurpers," and speaking of "wise limits" when referring to their future plans. They often deferred to men in their cooperative endeavors, which also revealed the tentative nature of newly charted directions. Most of the women who became active in the organizational life of the city were married, occupied a relatively elite status, and enjoyed their positions. While they believed certain changes should be made in the life of the city and fully intended to play a leading role in that process, social revolution was not on their agenda. They hoped to bring about reform within the existing social structure and in an atmosphere of domestic peace.

What remained constant throughout the decades of this study was the women's desire for female camaraderie, and the maintenance and expansion of homosocial interrelationships. There was an enthusiasm and vibrancy in the emerging sisterhood and a pride in the discovery of each other's capabilities and talents. Lide Meriwether and Elizabeth Saxon, who had so often cooperated in temperance and suffrage work, were referred to as "comrades in arms." The activism of Meriwether and Elizabeth Johnson was carried on by their daughters in the succeeding generation, establishing in those two families something of a tradition of female involvement. And among the general female population, there was recognition of the process of transmitting public responsibility from one generation to the next.

Women credited female organizational life with having "strengthened their mental force," which "inspired ambitions and courage in women." Florence Turner commented that: "One of the best values in club life is the training we get in discovering ourselves. . . . Club training teaches women to meet and master the exigencies of life — new problems and conditions have no terror for her."[1] Another woman commented "that when the history of the Nineteenth Century is written, it will be a history of the America undiscovered by Columbus. . . . Of women, broad in sympathy, tolerant in understanding and forming a most earnest, active chain, surrounding the continent."[2]

That women derived a great sense of self-fulfillment from their organizational experiences is clear. They felt more connected and integrated into the life of the city, which served as an antidote to a long-nagging sense of marginality and powerlessness. The female organizational impetus in Memphis contributed to the bonding of woman to woman; and through their network of clubs and organizations, Memphis women had indeed — to paraphrase Carroll Smith-Rosenberg — afforded each other mutual support, personal companionship, and a certain amount of social solidarity.[3]

Women's confidence in themselves and in each other had reached a high peak. Most women of this study, if polled in 1915, would have expressed great optimism about women's future. Proclaimed *Club Affairs*: "We are facing the dawn of a new day . . . the women of the twentieth century are beholding the advance of a better and brighter era for all humanity — the emancipation of women from the thraldom of the past."[4]

Women's efforts had been aimed basically at integrating individuals into the existing social structures, not at changing those structures. Most could comfortably attack alcohol as an evil that led to abuse in families, and could rally to the causes for helping women and children to deal with hopelessness, illness, and poverty. But these women reformers did not look critically at such things as women's position in marriage and the structure of the family, or women's lack of economic autonomy. Perhaps these would have been unreasonable expectations, as this particular group of women was just beginning to build the kind of support networks that could realistically sustain an assault on the hierarchy. As it was, the women believed they had been responsible for significant progress in shaping the future direction of their city and viewed themselves as crusaders. Through their own organized, determined, and persistent actions, they had achieved rights previously denied them.

As women's behavior changed, there had been some shifting in the male-female equation, and women experienced a heightened sense of self-respect, no longer perceiving themselves — or being perceived — as powerless beings. They were no longer silent or expected to be so, and *intelligence* and *competence* were replacing the more passive adjectives of female prescription. Yet, the basic argument that had allowed women an expanded role — the extension of her "natural" qualities into the public sphere — served ultimately to lock her into an ever-tightening straitjacket of equating reproductive function with life vocation. Ultimately, despite some shifting, there had been no appreciable change in the gender hierarchy, as these reforming women did not address the crucial and dangerous issues which lay at the heart of their role constraints. Change in behavior did not mean a permanent change in attitudes about the assigned spheres of men and women. While cast in a crusading image, these women were not revolutionaries, nor would they have wanted to risk a radical's punishment. They were content with what they had achieved and confident that over time the direction they had charted toward equality would continue. They failed to grasp the delicate nature of change and did not understand the influence of economics and politics in determining their future. They did not really grasp the complexities of the depths they had touched — that would be left for succeeding generations.

Notes

Introduction

1. Anne Firor Scott, *The Southern Lady, from Pedestal to Politics 1830–1930* (Chicago: University of Chicago Press, 1970), ix–xii.
2. Karen Blair, *The Clubwoman as Feminist* (New York: Holmes & Meier Publishers, 1980).
3. Jean Friedman, *The Enclosed Garden* (Chapel Hill: University of North Carolina Press, 1985), xi–xiii; 3–20.
4. Examples of such treatment are William Miller, *Memphis during the Progressive Era, 1900–1917* (Memphis: Memphis State University Press, 1975); J. P. Young, *Standard History of Memphis, Tennessee* (Knoxville: H. W. Crew and Co., 1912); Paul Coppock, *Memphis Sketches* (Friends of Memphis and Shelby County Libraries, 1976).
5. Gerald M. Capers, *Biography of a River Town* (Chapel Hill: University of North Carolina Press, 1939), 228.
6. Tim Mason, "Women in Germany, 1925–1940: Family, Welfare and Work," *History Workshop* 2 (Autumn 1976), 26.
7. See Elizabeth S. Hoyt, "Some Phases of the History of the Woman's Movement in Tennessee," (M.A. Thesis, University of Tennessee, 1931); A. Elizabeth Taylor, *The Woman Suffrage Movement in Tennessee* (New York: Bookman Associates, 1959); and Grace Elizabeth Prescott, "The Woman Suffrage Movement in Memphis: Its Place in the State, Sectional and National Movements," *West Tennessee Historical Society Papers*, No. 18 (1964), 87–106.
8. The most recent treatment of Frances Wright is Celia Morris Eckhardt, *Fanny Wright, Rebel in America* (Cambridge, Mass.: Harvard University Press, 1984).
9. Kathleen Christine Berkeley, "Elizabeth Avery Meriwether, 'An Advocate for Her Sex': Feminism and Conservatism in the Post-Civil War South," *Tennessee Historical Quarterly* 43 (Winter 1984), 390–406.

10.   "'The Ladies Want to Bring About Reform in the Public Schools': Public Education and Women's Rights in the Post-Civil War South," *History of Education Quarterly* 24 (Spring 1984), 45–58. See also Berkeley's "'Like a Plague of Locust': Immigration and Social Change in Memphis, Tennessee, 1850–1880" (Ph.D. diss., University of California, Los Angeles, 1980).

11.   The following statement of the Tennessee Federation of Women's Clubs on what constituted greatness in cities reflected a widely held female sentiment: "Cities are measured today more than ever by the happiness of their people, and that city is greatest which gives to its citizens the most in protection, education, recreation and beauty." See *Woman's Work in Tennessee* (Memphis: Printed under the auspices of the Tennessee Federation of Women's Clubs by Jones-Briggs Co., 1916), 267.

12.   Gerda Lerner, "Placing Women in History: Definitions and Challenges," *Feminist Studies* 3 (Fall 1975), 5–6.

13.   Alice Kessler-Harris, "Women's History on Trial," *The Nation*, 7 September 1985, 161.

14.   Quoted in Mary Ryan, *Womanhood in America* (New York: New Viewpoints, 1975), 10.

15.   Natalie Z. Davis, "Women's History in Transition: The European Case," *Feminist Studies* 3 (Spring/Summer 1976), 83–90.

16.   Anne Firor Scott, "The 'New Woman' in the New South," in *Making the Invisible Woman Visible* (Urbana: University of Illinois Press, 1984), 215.

Chapter 1. Beginnings of a Female Network

1.   See Bette Baird Tilly, "Aspects of Social and Economic Life in West Tennessee before the Civil War" (Ph.D. diss., Memphis State University, 1974), 326–29.

2.   Centennial Edition, *Memphis Commercial Appeal*, 1 January 1940.

3.   Ibid.; Young, 94.

4.   Ellen Davies-Rodgers, *The Great Book, Calvary Protestant Episcopal Church, 1832–1972* (Memphis: The Plantation Press, 1973), 573.

5.   Kathleen Berkeley, "'Like a Plague of Locust,'" 34.

6.   Quoted in Bessie Z. Jones, ed., *Hospital Sketches* (Cambridge, Mass.: Harvard University Press, Belknap Press, 1960), xviii.

7.   See Fred T. Wooten, Jr., "Religious Activity in Civil War Memphis," *West Tennessee Historical Quarterly* 3 (March–December 1944,) 131–149; Centennial Edition, *Memphis Commercial Appeal*, 1 January 1940.

8. Davies-Rodgers, *The Great Book*, 570–73, theorizes that Pope was the head of Calvary Parochial School, begun in 1847, which was one and the same as St. Mary's Episcopal School. She is described as "distinguished for her polish, refinement and literary taste," and was "proficient in Latin, Greek, German and Math." Pope was also a member of the Diocesan Missionary Society.

9. Centennial Edition, *Memphis Commercial Appeal*, 1 January 1940.

10. Ibid.

11. Mrs. S. E. D. Smith, *The Soldier's Friend* (Memphis: The Bulletin Publishing Co., 1867), 54.

12. J. M. Keating, *History of the City of Memphis* (Syracuse, N.Y.: D. Mason & Co., Publishers, 1888, repr., Memphis: Burke's Book Store and Frank and Gennie Myers, n.d.), 545.

13. "Woman's Edition," *Memphis Commercial Appeal*, 14 February 1895.

14. Elizabeth Meriwether's published fiction includes the following: *The Master of Red Leaf* (1873); *The Ku Klux Klan; Or the Carpet-Bagger of New Orleans* (1877); *Black and White, A Novel* (1881); *The Devil's Dance. A Play* (1886); *The Sowing of Swords, Or the Soul of the Sixties* (1910).

15. Berkeley, "Elizabeth Avery Meriwether," 390–406.

16. Berkeley, "'The Ladies Want to Bring About Reform,'" 45–58, contends the whole issue was "symptomatic of a society in transition."

17. From November 1872 through July 1873 *The Memphis Daily Appeal*'s pages were filled with comment and letters about this issue.

18. Quoted in Berkeley, "The Ladies Want to Bring About Reform," 51; *Memphis Daily Appeal*, 11 March 1873.

19. *Memphis Daily Appeal*, 2 February 1873.

20. Ibid., 3 February 1873. It was in the area of education that the women would make the most significant inroads in entering public life. The Women's Public School Association was formed in 1905, bringing about direct involvement with the board of education and school policies. In 1908 the Nineteenth Century Club began agitation that led to women being made eligible for the school board. In 1915 the Tennessee legislature enacted legislation granting women this right. The following year, two women were elected to the Memphis school board. See chapter 5.

21. *Memphis Daily Appeal*, 6, 7, 10 March; 11 April 1873.

22. See Berkeley, "The Ladies Want to Bring About Reform," 51.

23. *Woman's Work in Tennessee* (Memphis: Printed under the auspices of the Tennessee Federation of Women's Clubs by Jones-Briggs, Co., 1916), 267.

24. *The Gleaner*, June 1891, 121. A publication of the Memphis Women's Christian Association.

25. *Memphis Appeal-Avalanche,* 13 April 1890.

26. For the names of the trustees see J. P. Young, 431.

27. Henry C. Wiley, ed., *Biographical Cyclopaedia of American Women* (New York: The Halvord Publishing Co., Inc., 1928), 3:35; Young, 431.

28. *Memphis Appeal-Avalanche,* 13 April 1890.

29. Conway did have some very close relationships with women. She referred to one, "a brilliant woman" who had been to her "as Jonathan to David," and said they had been "companions in doubt" about their religious faith. N. M. Long, *Sermons and Addresses* (Memphis: S. C. Toof & Co., 1906), 272–73. Conway also made reference to a female companion with whom she traveled in Germany in 1904. They studied literature together, and Conway spoke of "our heart-to-hearts" and noted receiving letters "every day or two" after they had parted. Clara Conway, *Letters and Lyrics* (Memphis: privately printed, 1905), 31. She seems to have been more comfortable in the company of women, and it was with women and for women that she spent most of the meaningful efforts of her life. N. M. Long, pastor of the Strangers Congregational Church, of which Conway was a communicant, noted her "magnetic charm" and her ability to "stir with high ambition the frailest and most refined of maiden natures." Long described Conway as "more than a teacher," she was a "fervid prophetess." Long, 270.

30. Wiley, 35.

31. Clara Conway was born in New Orleans in 1844, the daughter of desperately poor Irish parents who had come to America in the early nineteenth century. Her father and grandfather were said to have lived in constant danger because of their Irish patriotism. Clara Conway was brought to Memphis about 1855, as both of her parents had died, and was placed in Saint Agnes School. Wiley, 32.

32. Conway, 35–36.

33. *Memphis Appeal-Avalanche,* 11 September 1890.

34. Ibid., 20 December 1889.

35. Ibid.

36. Ibid.

37. See chapter 2.

38. See chapter 4.

39. *Memphis Appeal-Avalanche,* 27 November 1892.

40. Wiley, 101.

41. Higbee said that eleven graduates of the Court Street Female High School were in the employ of the Memphis city schools as of 1872 to 1873. Twenty-Second Annual Report of the Board of Education for the City of Memphis, Tennessee, 1872–73 (Memphis, Tenn., 1873), Memphis Room, Memphis Public Library.

42. Wiley, 102.
43. Ibid.
44. Wiley, 104.
45. *Memphis Commercial Appeal,* 17 April 1897.
46. Ibid.
47. Elizabeth Meriwether was described as having come from "an old Tennessee family with the bluest blood of the sunny south coursing through their veins." "Sunday Sayings," Elizabeth Avery Meriwether scrapbook, Meriwether family papers, series IV, Mississippi Valley Collection, Memphis State University, Memphis, Tenn.; hereinafter cited as (MVC). Her father was a physician of Quaker origin and her maternal grandfather had been a rich Virginia planter who owned from seventy-five to eighty slaves and a large plantation. Her brother, Tom Avery, became a distinguished lawyer and United States congressman. Their sister, Amanda, married a wealthy Memphian named Trezevant. The Meriwether brothers were from a plantation-owning Kentucky family and were considered rich by the standards of that era.
48. Minor Meriwether resigned from the Southern Historical and Benevolent Association of St. Louis in 1884 because ladies were not allowed to attend meetings. Letter from Minor Meriwether to C. W. Sadler, 3 July 1884. Meriwether family papers, series I, MVC. When Lide Meriwether went to Nashville in 1888 to attend the Prohibition party's convention, her husband, Niles, urged her to get a woman suffrage plank, telling her that was the only way to win legislation in other areas such as girlhood protection and equal wages. *Union Signal,* 29 March 1888, 4.
49. Meriwether's parents were orthodox Methodists and obeyed the teachings very strictly. They had family prayers every morning after which her father read the Bible aloud. When her father said she should be thankful to God for her food, she thought she should be thankful "to her father who'd earned the money to buy the slave, 'Aunt Sally,' who cooked it." Elizabeth Avery Meriwether, typescript of *Recollections of 92 Years,* Meriwether family papers, series IV, MVC.
50. Elizabeth Avery Meriwether, *Recollections of 92 Years: 1824–1916* (Nashville: Tennessee Historical Commission, 1958), 8.
51. Ibid., 35.
52. "Proposed Lecture by Mrs. Meriwether," Elizabeth Avery Meriwether scrapbook, 46. Meriwether family papers, series IV, MVC.
53. Elizabeth Meriwether's husband was an officer in the Confederacy and had left her in Memphis to care for herself and two young children. Her memoirs poignantly depict her desperate struggles. Meriwether was ordered to leave the city by General William Sherman as part of a retaliation program for Confederate bombardment of federal gunboats in the Mississippi River and guerrilla harassment. Pregnant, she

and her family left Memphis in the midst of winter in search of her husband's company. Taken in by a woman in Columbus, Mississippi, she gave birth in December 1862 to her third child. She later wrote a story based on her experiences for a contest sponsored by a southern newspaper, the prize money being used to keep her children fed and clothed as her war struggles continued.

54. *The Tablet*, 27 January 1872. Meriwether family papers, series II, MVC. Unfortunately only two issues of *The Tablet* are known to exist.

55. Meriwether claimed proudly that the paper was profitable while she owned it. It was only after the two men took over that *The Tablet* failed, thus it was no woman's failure she explained. Meriwether, *Recollections*, 218–20.

56. Kathleen Berkeley contends that prior to the schoolteachers' wage dispute suffrage was a part of a package of reforms Meriwether advocated. See Berkeley, "Elizabeth Avery Meriwether," 403.

57. Elizabeth Cady Stanton, Susan B. Anthony, and Matilda Joslyn Gage, eds., *History of Woman Suffrage* (New York: Arno Press, 1969), 3:822.

58. Meriwether, *Recollections*, v–vi.

59. Ibid., vi.

60. *Memphis Daily Appeal*, 6 May 1876.

61. Ibid., 3 May 1876.

62. Ibid., 4 May 1876.

63. Ibid.

64. Ibid., 6 May 1876.

65. Letter from Elizabeth A. Meriwether to Avery and Rivers Meriwether, 15 May 1876. Meriwether family papers, correspondence, series I, MVC.

66. Elizabeth A. Meriwether scrapbook. Meriwether family papers, series IV, MVC.

67. *Memphis Daily Appeal*, 6 May 1876.

68. Lide Meriwether's daughter, Mrs. M. M. Betts, became deeply entrenched in the struggle for ratification of the Nineteenth Amendment in 1920. Betts was also a member of the Nineteenth Century Club and the Women's Christian Temperance Union.

69. Mattie Duncan Beard, *The W.C.T.U. in the Volunteer State* (Kingsport, Tenn.: Kingsport Press, Inc., 1962), 117.

70. Ibid.

71. Anne Firor Scott, "The Troy Female Seminary," in *Making the Invisible Woman Visible* (Urbana: University of Illinois Press, 1984), 80.

72. Scott sees education as a major force in the spread of feminism. Female seminaries, she believes, were important agents in developing female self-perception as well as providing institutional links among women beyond a single community. See Scott's "The Troy

Female Seminary," 67–75, and "What, Then, Is the American?," in *Making the Invisible Woman Visible*, 37–63. Suzanne Lebsock in *The Free Women of Petersburg: Status and Culture in a Southern Town, 1784–1860* (New York: W. W. Norton & Company, 1985), 205–6, also theorizes that it was education that made the difference in accounting for the founding of Petersburg's Female Orphan Asylum in 1813. Requiring a "broader stage" for the seriousness of purpose with which they had become infused, the founding of the asylum provided a partial solution and "marked the coming of age of Petersburg's first generation of educated women."

73.   "Working for Humanity," Elizabeth Avery Meriwether scrapbook, Meriwether family papers, series IV, MVC.

74.   Wilma Dykeman, *Tennessee Women, Past and Present* (Memphis: Tennessee Commission for the Humanities, 1977), 27–8.

75.   Frances E. Willard and Mary A. Livermore, eds. *A Woman of the Century* (Buffalo: Charles Wells Moulton, 1893, repr. Detroit: Gale Research Co., 1967), 498. Lide and Niles Meriwether had three daughters. One, Mrs. M. M. Betts, lived in Memphis and inherited her mother's social activism. Another, Virginia M. Davis, was widowed as a very young woman and subsequently studied medicine in New York at Dr. Emily Blackwell's college. Davis became resident physician at the New York Infant Asylum when she was twenty-four years old. The third daughter married and lived in Alabama, and very little is known about her life.

76.   For a full discussion of the themes in *Soundings*, see chapter 2.

77.   *Union Signal*, 1 December 1887.

78.   Kathryn Kish Sklar, *Catharine Beecher, A Study in American Domesticity* (New York: W. W. Norton & Company, Inc., 1976), xiv.

79.   Women's and Young Women's Christian Association, *Annual Directory*, 1902, 8.

Chapter 2. The Women's Christian Association

1.   Quoted in Marian Morton, "Temperance, Benevolence, and the City: The Cleveland Non-Partisan Women's Christian Temperance Union, 1874–1900," *Ohio History* 91 (1982), 64.

2.   Women and Young Women's Christian Association, *Annual Directory*, 1902, 7.

3.   Ibid., 44. In 1883 the Memphis WCA was incorporated, and in 1896 by amendment to the charter it was renamed the Women's and Young Women's Christian Association. This was an entirely separate organi-

zation from the Young Women's Christian Association of Memphis organized in 1922.

4.   Beard, 4.

5.   William S. Speer, *Sketches of Prominent Tennesseeans* (Nashville: Elbert B. Tavel, 1888), 322.

6.   Mary Willett Lyle, "Early Settlement of Memphis, Recollections of Mary Willett Lyle," *Memphis Historical Society Papers,* ESM 4, January 1917.

7.   Scott, "What, Then, Is the American?," in *Making the Invisible Woman Visible,* 57.

8.   Beard, 115.

9.   See Donald Matthews, *Religion in the Old South* (Chicago: University of Chicago Press, 1977), 101–23, 238–40; John Carl Ruoff, "Southern Womanhood 1865–1920: An Intellectual and Cultural Study" (Ph.D. diss., University of Illinois, 1976), 160–62, 168, 175; Nancy Cott, *The Bonds of Womanhood: "Woman's Sphere" in New England, 1790–1835* (New Haven: Yale University Press, 1978), 127–59; Jacquelyn Dowd Hall, *Revolt against Chivalry* (New York: Columbia University Press, 1979), 66–67; Anne Firor Scott, "Women, Religion and Social Change, 1830–1920," in *Making the Invisible Woman Visible,* 190–211; Scott, *The Southern Lady: From Pedestal to Politics 1830–1930* (Chicago: University of Chicago Press, 1970), 136–43; Noreen Dunn Tatum, *A Crown of Service: A Story of Woman's Work in the Methodist Episcopal Church, South, from 1873*–1940 (Nashville: Parthenon Press, 1960), 349–52.

10.   As Anne Scott points out "the public life of virtually every southern woman for forty years began in a church society." Participation in the church enabled them to "gain confidence and slowly emerge from the self-consciousness and fear which had bound them." Scott, "Women, Religion, and Social Change," 109. But evangelism proved to be a two-edged sword for women. While gender was not an obstacle to "being powerful in the Lord", and women did receive encouragement in making the world anew, the evangelical concept of the family also strengthened the ideal of female domesticity and reinforced a social structure characterized by male superiority. Jean Friedman in *The Enclosed Garden* (Chapel Hill: University of North Carolina Press, 1985), 9–20, contends evangelical religion was an important factor retarding the development of female support networks outside the family, thus preventing the development of a self-conscious feminism in the preindustrial South.

11.   As one woman said of Willard: "The first time I heard her I lay awake all night for sheer gladness. It was such a wonderful revelation to me that a woman like Miss Willard could exist. I thanked God and took courage for humanity." Anna Gordon, *The Life of Frances Wil-*

lard (Evanston, Ill.: National Woman's Christian Temperance Union Publishing House, 1912), 102. See also Ruth Bordin, *Woman and Temperance: The Quest for Power and Liberty, 1873–1900* (Philadelphia: Temple University Press, 1981), 67–71, on Willard's magnetism.

12. *The Gleaner*, February 1892, 58.

13. Beard, 113. The Johnsons owned a plantation where the Poplar Avenue viaduct now stands; in addition, J. Cummings Johnson was a cotton buyer and started the first cottonseed oil business in Memphis.

14. *Memphis Daily Appeal*, 23 February 1875.

15. Ibid.

16. The directors as listed in the *Memphis Daily Appeal*, 23 February 1875 were: N. W. Speers, E. M. Apperson, Henry Craft, Judge C. W. Heiskell, Judge J. O. Pierce, Milton P. Jarnigan, G. W. Jones, Charles Kortrecht, A. S. McNear, and W. L. Scott.

17. "Woman's Edition," *Commercial Appeal*, 14 February 1895.

18. Women's and Young Women's Christian Association, *Annual Directory*, 1902, 7.

19. *Memphis Daily Appeal*, 6 November 1875.

20. Blair, 106.

21. *Memphis Daily Appeal*, 28 February 1875.

22. Based on husbands' occupations, the WCA was an organization of local elites. Of the ten charter members, four husbands' professions can be identified: one bank president (J. R. Godwin); one plantation owner and cottonseed-oil mill owner (J. Cummings Johnson); one lawyer and investor in several business concerns (T. J. Latham); and one clergyman (Samuel Watson) who was described as being of "independent means largely through real estate transaction." Speer, 567. Of the women on the various boards of WCA projects through 1908, eight were married to men prominent in the cotton business (G. W. Fisher, W. B. Galbreath, L. W. Scarborough, W. W. Schoolfield, Napoleon Hill, G. W. McRae, W. W. Guy, and B. W. Haller); five were married to lawyers, four of whom became judges; and others were scattered in businesses such as banker (R. D. Frayser); physicians (R. W. Mitchell, also president of the Board of Health; E. Miles Willett); wholesale chemicals (P. P. Van Vleet); wholesale grocery business (J. N. Oliver); and railroad board members (S. L. Tate, L. B. McFarland). Two husbands were officers in the Taxing District (W. W. Guy and M. Burke), two had been mayors of the city (J. R. Flippin and D. P. Hadden), and one a state legislator (Lois Bejach).

23. "Woman's Edition," *Memphis Commercial Appeal*, 14 February 1895.

24. Morton, 64.

25. By 1902 board membership was composed of eight women from each branch of the association and eight from the membership at large.

Twenty-Seventh Annual Directory of the Women's and Young Women's Christian Association (Memphis: Wills and Crumpton Printers, 1902).

26. *Memphis Daily Appeal*, 6 March 1881.
27. Women's and Young Women's Christian Association, *Annual Directory*, 1905–06, 47.
28. There were four women involved in WCA work who had been Southern Mothers during the Civil War and who remained active in its postbellum form, which was first called the Ladies Memorial Association and then the Ladies Confederate Historical Association. See Young, 566.
29. *The Gleaner*, February 1892, 58.
30. "Woman's Edition," *Memphis Commercial Appeal*, 14 February 1895.
31. *Daily Memphis Avalanche*, 27 February 1880.
32. *Memphis Daily Appeal*, 2 June 1883.
33. *Daily Memphis Avalanche*, 27 February 1880.
34. Ibid.
35. Ibid., 20 June 1880.
36. Mark David Connelly in *The Response to Prostitution in the Progressive Era* (Chapel Hill: University of North Carolina Press, 1980), 10, has noted the general confusion and imprecision that existed in attempting to define prostitution in the late nineteenth century. In the popular mind, as he points out, prostitution was a label often applied to "any premarital or non-monogamous female sexual activity, whether or not financial exchange was involved. Thus . . . potentially all sexual activity unsanctioned by marriage could be characterized as prostitution." Reading the comments of Memphians regarding the problem, it would appear that the WCA was dealing primarily with naive young girls, rather than hardened women who made a business of sexual activity.
37. Women's and Young Women's Christian Association, *Annual Directory*, 1902, 8.
38. *Daily Memphis Avalanche*, 6 March 1881; Women's and Young Women's Christian Association, *History-By-Laws*, Memphis, Tenn., 1952, 8.
39. *Daily Memphis Avalanche*, 29 June 1881.
40. *Memphis Daily Appeal*, 23 June 1889.
41. Ibid.
42. *Women's and Young Women's Christian Association Yearbook, 1892–93*.
43. *Daily Memphis Avalanche*, 6 March 1881.
44. *Memphis Daily Appeal*, 19 June 1883; 17 June 1884.
45. *Women's and Young Women's Christian Association Yearbook, 1892–93*.
46. In 1900 the Children's Home was merged into the Leath Orphan Asylum.
47. *The Gleaner*, March 1882, 76.

48. Ibid.
49. *Memphis Daily Appeal,* 19 June 1883.
50. *The Gleaner,* January 1892.
51. *Memphis Daily Appeal,* 22 January 1882.
52. The Johnsons were indeed the "angels" of the Mission Home. There are frequent references to their generosity: See Women and Young Women's Christian Association Annual Directories, 1902–6, 12; "Women's Edition," *Memphis Commercial Appeal,* 14 February 1895. In 1881, of $4,488.53 received by the Mission Home, $1,695 was said to have been donated by one person. It seems likely that this was Elizabeth Johnson. *Memphis Daily Avalanche,* 15 June 1881.
53. J. Cummings Johnson donated a lot on Myrtle Street as a possible future site for a home. "Woman's Edition," *Memphis Commercial Appeal,* 14 February 1895.
54. *Memphis Commercial Appeal,* 13 December 1908.
55. From 1923 to 1937 the Community Fund gave some financial support to the Ella Oliver Refuge, but decreasing numbers of applicants led to the withdrawal of those funds. In 1937 the Catholic church bought the building for a school for black children. Women and Young Women's Christian Association, *History-By-Laws,* 1952, 6.
56. See especially the sketch, "Guilty or Not Guilty?," *Soundings* (Memphis: Boyle and Chapman Publishers, 1872), 151–59.
57. Ibid., 153–54.
58. Ibid., 97.
59. See especially, "Am I My Brother's Keeper?," 8–18; and "The Hill Difficulty," 161–71, *Soundings.*
60. Ibid., 157.
61. Ibid., 14.
62. Ibid., 162.
63. Ibid., 160–61.
64. Ibid., 162.
65. Ibid., 167.
66. Ibid., 30. The theme of the "fallen woman" in Meriwether's book brings to mind two much later novels of Theodore Dreiser — *Sister Carrie* (1900) and *Jennie Gerhardt* (1911) — with which there are some striking similarities. Despite such characteristics as generosity, faithfulness, and love displayed by female characters in all three works, a hardboiled society rejected and punished them because they exercised their sexuality in an unorthodox way. Both of Dreiser's novels were attacked for their immorality, which gives one an added sense of how daring Meriwether's publication of *Soundings* would have been some thirty years earlier in 1872.
67. *Soundings,* 155–56.

68. Ibid., 98.
69. Ibid., 27.
70. The Home of the Good Shepherd addressed the needs of wayward girls, which was the extent of its focus. It was run by an order of Roman Catholic nuns and did not involve the efforts of private, lay citizens. The Home of the Good Shepherd began its work in Memphis in 1875.
71. Connelly, 7.
72. Ibid., 46.
73. Ibid., 7.
74. Cott, 152.
75. *Soundings*, 12.
76. "Woman's Edition," *Memphis Commercial Appeal*, 14 February 1895.
77. A lease was taken at 306 Second Street and donations provided for a matron, Mrs. S. A. Surprise. Women and Young Women's Christian Association, *Annual Directories*, 1902–6, 16.
78. Ibid.
79. "Woman's Edition," *Memphis Commercial Appeal*, 14 February 1895.
80. *Women's and Young Women's Christian Association Yearbook, 1892–93*.
81. Prosperity and optimism about the city's future had returned in the decade of the 1880s. From 1880 to 1890, population had increased from 33,592 to 50,313, and by 1900 would reach 102,000. The city government under the Taxing District was highly praised for its efficiency, and by the mid-1880s debt settlement had been achieved. As the decade came to a close a great sense of promise was expressed by Memphis citizens. See *Memphis Appeal-Avalanche*, 9 November, 18 December, 30 December 1890; "Memphis Past, Present and Future," *Commercial and Statistical Review of the City of Memphis, Tennessee* (n.p. Reilly and Thomas, 1883); Young, 213.
82. Women's and Young Women's Christian Association, *Annual Directory*, 1902, 16.
83. *Memphis Daily Appeal*, 14 April 1889.
84. Ibid., 14 April 1890.
85. *Women's and Young Women's Christian Association Yearbook, 1892–93*.
86. *Memphis Daily Appeal*, 21 May 1890.
87. *The Gleaner*, March 1892, 69.
88. Ibid., June 1892, 42.
89. *Women's and Young Women's Christian Association Yearbook, 1892–93*.
90. *The Gleaner*, June 1891, 40.
91. *Memphis Daily Appeal*, 23 June 1889.
92. A local minister said of women's charitable efforts: "Her place in the Church and in all works of charity, where suffering was to be relieved,

could not be filled except by her." *Memphis Daily Appeal,* 19 June 1883.

93. "Woman's Edition," *Memphis Commercial Appeal,* 14 February 1895.

94. The committee of the board of directors consisted of Mrs. Watson, president of the WCA, who had succeeded Mrs. Johnson; Mrs. Austin; and Mrs. Schoolfield. On the men's advisory committee were some of the city's most prominent businessmen: Dr. D. T. Porter, J. S. Menken, J. C. Day, Napoleon Hill, and J. R. Godwin.

95. *Memphis Daily Appeal,* 14 December 1889; 20 May 1890; *Memphis Appeal-Avalanche,* 15 December 1890.

96. Women's and Young Women's Christian Association, *Annual Directory,* 1902, 19.

97. Ibid., 26.

98. *Commercial Appeal,* 1 January 1940. In 1970 the building was sold for urban renewal and demolished. Paul Coppock, *Memphis Sketches* (Friends of Memphis and Shelby County Libraries, 1976), 148.

99. *Memphis Daily Appeal,* 25 May 1890.

100. *Memphis Daily Appeal,* 25 May 1890.

101. William Leach has argued that a combination of ethnic, regional, political, and economic factors prevented the general feminist movement from achieving true equality within the sexual relation. And, at the root of the feminist failure to create a new social ideology was the possessive individualism of the democratic liberal tradition. See William Leach, *True Love and Perfect Union: The Feminist Reform of Sex and Society* (New York: Basic Books, 1980), epilogue.

102. *The Gleaner,* January 1892, 42.

103. Ibid.

104. Quoted in Scott, *The Southern Lady,* 124.

105. *Memphis Daily Appeal,* 20 May, 1890.

106. The annual dues of two dollars was the same for all three categories.

107. *Commercial and Statistical Review,* 74.

108. Ibid. *The Gleaner* was published for ten years. The only copies known to exist are in the Memphis Public Library, Memphis, Tennessee.

109. *Memphis Daily Appeal,* 15 July 1884.

110. Young, 221.

111. *Memphis Daily Appeal,* 15 July 1881; 14 February 1882; 7 October 1883; 15 July 1884.

112. *Daily Memphis Avalanche,* 20 January 1880.

113. The Christmas Club was formed in 1887 under the leadership of J. S. Menken, a Jewish merchant and owner of Menken's Department Store. Originally operating during the Christmas season and focusing attention upon the needs of the poor for food and toys, the club expanded into a permanent organization using whatever surplus funds

it had to minister to the needs of indigent Memphians. In 1893 much philanthropic work, including the Christmas Club, was united under the banner of the United Charities. Although many of the city's women were actively involved, men held most leadership positions. See "Women's Edition," *Memphis Commercial Appeal*, 14 February 1895; *Memphis Daily Appeal*, 10 December 1889.

114. See Lebsock, 228–31.

Chapter 3. The Woman's Christian Temperance Union

1. Young, 215.
2. Women from eighteen different states were involved in the formation of the WCTU. Beard, 23.
3. Belle Kearney, *A Slaveholder's Daughter* (New York: Abbey Press, 1900), 113.
4. As Bordin, 13, points out, political means were used by the WCTU from the start and legislative solutions were never eschewed. But it was with the elevation of Frances Willard to the presidency that the focus in this direction became more persistent.
5. *The Issue*, 22 September 1887. Official organ of the Tennessee State Temperance Alliance, Tennessee Good Templars, Woman's Christian Temperance Union. Tennessee State Library and Archives, Nashville, Tennessee.
6. Philip M. Hamer, *Tennessee, a History, 1673–1932* (New York: The American Historical Society, 1933), 2:735.
7. *Memphis Daily Appeal*, 23 February 1876.
8. Ibid., 10 March 1876.
9. Ibid., 14 March 1876.
10. Beard, 114.
11. Ibid.
12. Report of the Committee on Southern Work, 6th Annual Convention, WCTU, 1879, 61. Temperance and Prohibition Papers, WCTU Series. The Michigan Historical Collections, The Ohio Historical Society, The Woman's Christian Temperance Union (Ann Arbor: University of Michigan, 1977).
13. See Bordin, 99–116, for a discussion of the expanded philanthropic range of WCTU activities.
14. Bordin, 15.
15. *Union Signal*, 4 March 1886, 10.
16. Elizabeth Putnam Gordon, *Women Torch Bearers* (Evanston, Ill.: National Woman's Christian Temperance Union Publishing House, 1924), 19.

17. Quoted in Scott, "Women, Religion, and Social Change in the South, 1830–1930," 204.
18. *Union Signal*, 8 September 1887.
19. Minutes, 9th Annual Convention, WCTU, 1882, 34–41. Temperance and Prohibition Papers, WCTU Series.
20. Minutes, 14th Annual Convention, WCTU, 1887, 136.
21. Quoted in Beard, 5.
22. The Hope Night School was begun by Elizabeth Johnson's husband, J. C. Johnson, who started night classes for orphan boys who roamed the streets after the 1878 yellow-fever epidemic. Lillian Johnson, the daughter of Elizabeth and J. C. Johnson, carried on the school when her father left Memphis in 1887. The Hope Night School was incorporated into the Memphis city schools in 1892.
23. Memphis WCTU officers for 1895 were: Mary Abernathy, president; Lide Meriwether, recording secretary; Dr. Louise Droillard, corresponding secretary; Ada Waddell, treasurer. All were active in WCA work as well. "Woman's Edition," *Memphis Commercial Appeal*, 14 February 1895.
24. Grieving deeply over the death of her sister in 1881, Meriwether left Memphis to spend some time with a friend in Arkansas. While visiting, Meriwether accompanied her friend to a WCTU state convention. To that time, she had given prohibition little thought. But at this convention Meriwether "awakened to the cause" and returned to Tennessee where she became heavily involved in temperance work and a leading figure in the WCTU. *Union Signal*, 16 February 1886; 1 December 1887.
25. Clipping, Lyle Saxon papers, Department of Manuscripts, Tulane University, New Orleans, Louisiana.
26. Saxon's only daughter, Ina Saxon Murray, lived in Memphis. Saxon died in Memphis in 1915 at the age of 82.
27. Elizabeth Lyle Saxon, *A Southern Woman's War Time Reminiscences* (Memphis, Tenn.: Press of the Pilcher Printing Co., 1905), 24.
28. Saxon's father descended from a long line of tyranny-hating Irish, the first having come to America in 1745. Her father's full name, Andrew Jackson Lyle, also suggests the family's admiration for one viewed as an adversary of the intrenched interests.
29. Willard and Livermore, 634; Elizabeth Lyle Saxon, *Poems of Elizabeth Lyle Saxon* (Dallas: Clyde C. Cockrell Co., 1932), 9.
30. Saxon's poems were published under the *nom de plume*, Annette Lyle. Her short stories and sketches appeared in the Louisville, Kentucky, *Courier;* Columbia, South Carolina, *Banner;* and the Philadelphia *Courier.*
31. "Mrs. Saxon's Wartime Reminiscences," manuscript, Lyle Saxon papers.

32. Ibid.
33. Saxon, *A Southern Woman's War Time Reminiscences*, 31, 39–40.
34. Ibid., 14.
35. Stanton, et al., 3:188.
36. Ibid., 794.
37. Ibid.
38. Minutes, 12th Annual Convention WCTU, 1885, 116.
39. Saxon, *Poems*, 11.
40. "E. L. Saxon's Address before the Constitutional Convention of the State of Louisiana," clipping, Lyle Saxon collection.
41. Willard and Livermore, 625.
42. "A Woman's Work. Letter from Mrs. E. L. Saxon," clipping, Lyle Saxon papers.
43. "Mrs. Saxon's Wartime Reminiscences," manuscript, Lyle Saxon papers.
44. Ibid.
45. Saxon, *A Southern Woman's War Time Reminiscences*, 24.
46. "Mrs. Saxon's Wartime Reminiscences," manuscript, Lyle Saxon papers.
47. "A Woman's Work. Letter from Mrs. E. L. Saxon," clipping, Lyle Saxon papers.
48. *Memphis Daily Appeal*, 30 April 1884.
49. Saxon was awarded the Clara Conway Memorial Membership in the Nineteenth Century Club in 1908 and was chairman of the Department of History and Philanthropy. She would also be made an honorary member of the Confederate Memorial Association, the Harvey Mathes Chapter of the United Daughters of the Confederacy, and the Press and Author's Club.
50. *The Issue*, 22 September 1887.
51. "Supremacy of Women," clipping, Lyle Saxon papers.
52. Beard, 8.
53. Minutes, 14th Annual Convention, WCTU, 1887, 136. Membership in some of the unions was extremely small. In Milan, Tennessee, for example, the minutes reveal that from 1896 to 1899 attendance at monthly meetings ranged from as few as five to as many as thirteen. The membership list for 1898 recorded thirteen members, nine honorary members (male), and fifteen Young Women's Christian Temperance Union members. Nonetheless, when asked what good they had derived from joining and working in the WCTU, "all expressed themselves as being strengthened in the cause of temperance and benefited in many ways." One member stated she "had been strengthened in working and knowing there were so many good and noble women working with her." Minute Book, Milan WCTU, 14 May 1896.
54. *Union Signal*, 24 February 1887.
55. Bordin, 79.

56. Educated in one of South Carolina's best ladies' academies, Sallie Chapin performed her first public service in the Confederacy's Soldier's Relief Society and subsequently became president of the Ladies Christian Association. The widow of a prominent Charleston merchant, she became involved in WCTU work and by 1881 was lecturing and organizing widely. See Edward James, ed., *Notable American Women* (Cambridge: Harvard University Press, 1971), 1:321–22.

57. Frances Willard, *Women and Temperance* (New York: Arno Press, 1972), 547.

58. Bordin, 82.

59. Beard, 8.

60. *Union Signal*, 4 March 1886.

61. Ibid., 18 November 1887.

62. Willard, *Woman and Temperance*, 551–52.

63. *Union Signal*, 7 October 1886.

64. In addition to Phillips the officers were: Corresponding secretary, Mrs. T. A. Sykes, Nashville, whose husband was a state legislator; recording secretary, Mrs. Martha Young, McKenzie; treasurer, Mrs. A. B. Kenny, Ripley, whose husband was a minister.

65. Minutes, 14th Annual Convention, WCTU, 1887, 137.

66. Paul Isaac, *Prohibition and Politics: Turbulent Decades in Tennessee, 1885–1920* (Knoxville: University of Tennessee Press, 1965), 10–11.

67. Ibid., 12–13.

68. John Trotwood Moore, *Tennessee, the Volunteer State, 1769–1923* (Chicago: S. J. Clarke Publishing Co., 1923), 1:798.

69. Minutes, 14th Annual Convention, WCTU, 1887, 136.

70. Ibid.

71. *Memphis Daily Appeal*, 30 September 1887.

72. Grace Leab, "The Temperance Movement in Tennessee, 1860–1907" (M. A. thesis, University of Tennessee, 1938), 50; *Memphis Daily Appeal*, 30 September 1887.

73. Quoted in Isaac, 78.

74. "Woman's Edition," *Memphis Commercial Appeal*, 14 February 1895.

75. See Yao Foli Modey, "The Struggle over Prohibition in Memphis, 1880–1930" (Ph.D. diss., Memphis State University, 1983), 8–9, 15–21.

76. Minutes, 14th Annual Convention, WCTU, 1887, appendix, ccxxiv.

77. Leab, 74.

78. Moore, 799.

79. *Memphis Commercial Appeal*, 23 November 1908.

80. Modey, 121–23.

81. Isaac, 165–66.

82. Quoted in Isaac, 255.

83. Ibid., 39–42.

84.   The departments were: Juvenile Work, Prison Work, Legislative Work, Religious Bodies, Colored People, Press Work, Young Women's Work, State and County Fairs, Work among Foreigners, Heredity and Hygiene, Unfermented Wine, *Union Signal* and *The Issue,* Sunday Work, Relation of Temperance to Labor, Mothers and Meetings, Promotion of Social Purity. Five departments were headed by Memphis women: Dr. Rachel Gowling, Mrs. J. C. Johnson, Mrs. Lide Meriwether, Mrs. Mary Abernathy, and Mrs. Bettie Hill.

85.   "Woman's Edition," *Memphis Commercial Appeal,* 14 February 1895.

86.   "Age of Consent," clipping, Lyle Saxon papers.

87.   Willard had personally endorsed woman suffrage in 1876 when she made a "home protection" speech to the Newark convention. After becoming president of the WCTU in 1879, she used her office to appeal for suffrage in her annual addresses. Many northern members had long believed suffrage necessary to secure the passage and enforcement of prohibition laws. In 1881 a franchise department was added to the national organization at their annual convention in Washington, D.C., and the "home protection" ballot was adopted. The nine southern states represented there declined to participate either in the discussions or in the vote. In 1894 the national WCTU made an official commitment based on natural rights — having moved beyond the original "home protection" argument. Local unions enjoyed autonomy, however, which left them room for nonparticipation. It was not until 1885 that woman suffrage was endorsed by the Memphis WCTU, and not until well into the twentieth century that it became widely accepted there. See Bordin, 119–20; *The Issue,* 9 February 1888.

88.   *Memphis Daily Appeal,* 21 February, 1 April 1886; Grace Prescott, "The Woman Suffrage Movement in Memphis: Its Place in the State, Sectional and National Movements," *West Tennessee Historical Society Papers,* No. 18 (1964), 91.

89.   Minutes, 14th Annual Convention, WCTU, 1887, Appendix ccxxiv.

90.   *Union Signal,* 13 October 1887.

91.   *Union Signal,* 29 March 1888.

92.   *Memphis Commercial Appeal,* 2 May 1915. A separate suffrage organization was formed in Memphis on May 21, 1889, at the home of Mrs. A. D. Langstaff, and was called the Memphis Equal Rights Association. Lide Meriwether was the group's first president, and the forty-five women involved pledged to seek equal rights for women. While interest in suffrage grew throughout the nineteenth century, it was not until the second decade of the twentieth century that Memphis women in any significant numbers worked for the franchise as a separate and independent goal. Some women who played a role in

the WCA, WCTU, and Nineteenth Century Club also became suf-
fragists, and woman suffrage was another issue that contributed to
a developing sense of camaraderie and sisterhood among the women
in this study. However, until about 1915, woman suffrage remained
controversial among the women, and many still viewed it as too
radical. It was in the late teens of the twentieth century that suffrage
took hold in Memphis, and Tennessee was the final battleground upon
which the struggle for ratification of the Nineteenth Amendment was
at last won in 1920. Thus, chronologically, suffrage as a separate issue
lies beyond the scope of this study. For an account of suffrage in Memphis see Elizabeth S. Hoyt, "Some Phases of the History of the
Woman's Movement in Tennessee," (M. A. Thesis, University of Tennessee, 1931); A. Elizabeth Taylor, *The Woman Suffrage Movement
in Tennessee* (New York: Bookman Associates, 1959); and Grace
Elizabeth Prescott, "The Woman Suffrage Movement in Memphis:
Its Place in the State, Sectional and National Movements," *West Tennessee Historical Society Papers,* No. 18 (1964), 87–106.

93. *Memphis Commercial Appeal,* 2 May 1915.
94. Barbara L. Epstein. *The Politics of Domesticity: Women, Evangeli-
calism, and Temperance in Nineteenth Century America* (Middletown,
Conn.: Wesleyan University Press, 1981), 134–36.
95. Bordin, 162.
96. *Union Signal,* 16 February 1888.
97. Ibid., 10 March 1887.

Chapter 4. The Nineteenth Century Club

1. Carroll Smith-Rosenberg, "The Female World of Love and Ritual:
Relations between Women in Nineteenth Century America," *Signs*
1 (Autumn 1975), 9, 1–29.
2. On the development of women's clubs in Memphis see Annah Robinson Watson, "Development of the Club Idea in Memphis," *Mid-
Continent Magazine* 6 (1895), 152; *Club Life* November 1925, 34–35;
The South Today 1, no. 3 (October 1910), 6; *Memphis Commercial
Appeal* 10 February 1895, 1 January 1940; *Woman's Work in Tennessee,* 229.
3. Selden had been a founding member of the Thackeray Book Club,
the Free Kindergarten Association and the Memphis Woman's
Suffrage Association. She was a native Memphian and was educated
at Miss Mary Pope's School and at St. Mary's Episcopal School. *Social
Register of Memphis* 1925 (Memphis: Penn-Renshaw [1925]), 99.
4. *Memphis Commercial Appeal,* 12 November 1950.

5.   Hugh Higbee Huhn, *Biographical Notes, A Scrapbook*, 15. Memphis Room, Memphis Public Library.

6.   Robert C. Brinkley had extensive real estate holdings in Memphis, was a leading promotor of railroads, and built the Peabody Hotel. The *Nashville Banner* had said of Brinkley in 1850: Memphis can boast of a single citizen who . . . has aided public enterprise more liberally in proportion to his wealth than perhaps any individual in the South. Quoted in Young, 83.

7.   The founding members of the Nineteenth Century Club were: Mrs. Mary L. Beecher, Miss Clara Conway, Mrs. C. C. Currier, Mrs. Enoch Ensley, Mrs. Walter M. Farrabee, Mrs. John C. Judah, Mrs. William Katzenbarger, Mrs. R. J. Morgan, Mrs. Elizabeth B. Norton, Mrs. R. C. Patterson, Mrs. Clarence Selden, Mrs. Lavinia F. Selden, Mrs. Thomas M. Scruggs, Mrs. Bolton Smith, and Mrs. James Watson. The founders represented an impressive array of wealth, education, and social prominence. The professions represented by their spouses were those of the cotton business, investment banker, plantation owner, legal, and judicial. The civic activities of the women themselves were quite numerous. Mary Jamison Judah was the founder of the Memphis Woman's Club and Mary Beecher, who had been a Southern Mother, was also a charter member of that club. Mary Ensley, who was Beecher's daughter, was very active in the Women's Hospital Association. Of Mrs. Robert Morgan it was said, "Few ladies in Tennessee have better claims to be called intellectual," Quoted in Speer, 202. And Clara Conway was among the best known of the city's educators and writers. Grace Smith was a Wellesley graduate with such broad civic involvement that she and her husband were said to be leaders "in every liberal and cultural movement in the city." *Memphis Commercial Appeal*, 14 October 1932. Elise Selden was active in numerous organizations. See note 3.

8.   In Knoxville, where a woman's club had been formed in 1885, the word *club* had been purposely avoided and the organization named Ossoli Circle. See Ruoff, 167.

9.   "Souvenir," 20th Annual Congress, Association for the Advancement of Women, Memphis, 1892, 16.

10.   Clipping, Turner family scrapbook, in the possession of Mrs. Carroll Turner, Memphis, Tennessee.

11.   *First Annual Announcement*, Nineteenth Century Club, Memphis, 1890–91, 23.

12.   Clipping, Turner family scrapbook. Florence Acree Turner, a native Memphian, was educated at the Clara Conway Institute — where she later became a faculty member — and described Conway as an advisor "in nearly everything." Turner, at Conway's urging, studied art in

New York and became an active promoter of the arts in Memphis. She married B. F. Turner in 1890. She was president of the Nineteenth Century Club in 1903 and was later closely identified with efforts to control pollution caused by coal smoke in Memphis. Mayor Rowlett Paine appointed Turner to head a committee to work on solutions to this problem, and she received much credit for the growth of the use of gas in Memphis industry. Florence Acree Turner, "Pages from the Memoirs of Mrs. B. F. Turner," in the possession of Mrs. Carroll Turner, Memphis, Tennessee; *Memphis Press Scimitar*, 18 August 1952.

13. The other committees were Education, Literature and Art, and Purchasing. *First Annual Announcement*, Nineteenth Century Club, Memphis, 1890–91.

14. "Souvenir," 7–8.

15. There is disagreement over the genesis of the shift from awareness to activism within the women's club movement. Blair, 73–74, claims that the Women's Educational and Industrial Union, founded in 1877 in Boston, provides the model for the activist club. Lana Ruegamer, "'The Paradise of Exceptional Women': Chicago Women Reformers, 1863–1893" (Ph.D. diss., Indiana University, 1982), 175, accuses Blair of eastern myopia and credits the Chicago Woman's Club, founded in 1876, as being the municipal-housekeeping prototype.

16. Annah Robinson Watson, "Development of the Club Idea in Memphis," *Mid-Continent Magazine* 6 (1895), 153.

17. *75th Anniversary Volume*, Nineteenth Century Club, 1890–1965, 2.

18. *Art Supplement to the Greater Memphis Edition of the Press Scimitar*, April 1899, 57–58.

19. Watson, 144.

20. The Association for the Advancement of Women had been organized in 1873 "to consider and present practical methods for securing to women higher intellectual, moral, and physical conditions, with a view to the improvement of all domestic and social relations." Early club women believed it was essential to inspire other women to form organizations, and the Association for the Advancement of Women held congresses annually in different cities hoping to inspire the creation of socially active clubs all over the country. Ironically, as they succeeded in doing so, membership in the association declined as individual cities developed their own women's groups. The Association for the Advancement of Women held its last congress in 1897. See Blair, 45–56.

21. "Souvenir," 8.

22. Gerald M. Capers, *Biography of a River Town* (Chapel Hill: The University of North Carolina Press, 1939), 228.

23. William D. Miller, *Memphis during the Progressive Era, 1900–1917* (Memphis: Memphis State University Press, 1957).

24. Jane Cunningham Croly, *Sorosis: Its Origin and History* (New York: J. J. Little, 1886; repr., New York: Arno Press, 1975), 7.

25. Elise Selden was in New York at the time that the General Federation of Women's Clubs was organized. As she visited a women's club at that time she would certainly have been aware of plans for the federation's formation.

26. From 1890–1900 the Nineteenth Century Club occupied rooms in several locations in downtown Memphis. The first site was a room in the Collier Building at Main and Jefferson. They subsequently occupied space in the Planters Insurance Building, the Randolph Building, and the Lyceum before buying a clubhouse in 1900 at 174 N. Third Street, formerly LaSalette Academy for girls, thus becoming one of the first women's clubs in the nation to own its own home. In 1926 the club purchased its present location at 1433 Union Avenue. They financed the purchase with a $120,000 first-mortgage bond issue. See *20th Annual Announcement 1910–11*, Nineteenth Century Club, Memphis, Tennessee, 6; "Confidential Memorandum Dealing with the Nineteenth Century Club of Memphis, Tennessee," April 19, 1939.

27. Clipping, Turner family scrapbook.

28. The Nineteenth Century Club became an affiliate of the General Federation of Women's Clubs in 1891.

29. *Memphis Appeal-Avalanche*, 16 November 1892.

30. "Woman's Edition," *Memphis Commercial Appeal*, 14 February 1895.

31. Ossoli Circle had been founded in 1885 through the initiative of Mrs. Lizzie Crozier French, an active suffragist, and thirteen other women, in order "to stimulate intellectual and moral development, and to strengthen individual effort by organization." The first president, Mary Boyce Temple, was a Vassar graduate and was Ossoli's delegate to the meeting in New York City at which the General Federation of Women's Clubs was organized. The Ossoli Circle sponsored traveling libraries in Tennessee, was involved in mountain-school work, initiated the movement for the state Vocational School for Girls, as well as seeking improvement in the legal status of women. See Ruoff, 167; *Women's Work in Tennessee*, 210, 245.

32. Hamer, 2:715.

33. *Woman's Work in Tennessee*, 21. Subsequent presidents of the Tennessee Federation of Women's Clubs who also served as presidents of the Nineteenth Century Club, although not simultaneously, were: 1902, Mrs. Kellar Anderson; 1905, Mrs. A. S. Buchanan; 1908, Mrs. James R. McCormack; 1913, Mrs. Isaac Reese.

34. *Club Affairs*, February 1917, 9.

35. Minutes, Legislative Council, 19 January 1893, 46.
36. Young, 236.
37. Of the eighteen officers or heads of committees of the Law and Order League, eight had wives who were Nineteenth Century Club members. Of these eight wives, one would serve as president of the Nineteenth Century Club, one had been a founding member, and one served on the governing board.
38. Clipping, Turner family scrapbook.
39. *Memphis Commercial Appeal*, 8 November 1908.
40. Minnie Walter was from Holly Springs, Mississippi, and her forefathers were described as "philanthropists" and people of "large interests." She was said to have been given "every educational advantage." In 1873 she married Henry Myer, who served as secretary of state for Mississippi. Upon his retirement from politics in 1881, they moved to Memphis where he became involved in the mortgage-loan business. Minnie Myer became an ardent advocate of women's clubs. *Woman's Work in Tennessee*, 275.
41. *Memphis Commercial Appeal*, 6 February 1895.
42. Ibid., 13 December 1907.
43. The Housekeepers' Club had become a model for other cities throughout Tennessee, Mississippi, and Arkansas. *Woman's Work in Tennessee*, 275.
44. *Memphis Commercial Appeal*, 8 November 1908.
45. L. B. McFarland was born in Somerville, Tennessee, and came to live in Memphis after the Civil War in order to practice law. His first partner was Robert J. Morgan, whose wife was a founding member of the Nineteenth Century Club. McFarland became a very successful railroad lawyer and served on several railroad company boards of directors. His first wife was from a prominent Alabama family, and after her death in 1900 McFarland married Floy Graham Allen, a Memphis native whose family had been among the city's early settlers and became large land owners. Floy McFarland was an active member of the Nineteenth Century Club. L. B. McFarland, *Memoirs and Addresses*, n.p., n.d., 10–14; *Memphis Social Register 1925*, 81.
46. McFarland, 119.
47. The women were well aware of the importance of male allies in high places. Dr. B. F. Turner, a prominent Memphis physician, headed the Sanitary Science Committee; Dr. J. L. Andrews, president of the Memphis Department of Health in 1908, headed the Sanitary Laundry Committee; and Israel Peres, who had been president of the Memphis school board, headed the Personal and Public Hygiene Committee. *Memphis Commercial Appeal*, 8 November 1908. The wives of Turner and Andrews were also Nineteenth Century Club members. See note 12 for Florence Turner.

48. *Club Life*, November 1925, 17.
49. "Report to the Tennessee Federation of Women's Clubs," Minutes, Nineteenth Century Club, 10 April 1910.
50. Minutes, Nineteenth Century Club, 1 May 1908; 7 October 1914; 6 November 1916.
51. *Memphis Commercial Appeal*, 14, 20 April 1917.
52. Clipping, scrapbook, Nineteenth Century Club.
53. Clipping, Lyle Saxon papers, Department of Manuscripts, Tulane University, New Orleans, La.
54. Lizzie Crozier French, founder of Ossoli Circle, had been instrumental in securing a police matron for Knoxville in 1890. She was aided in her efforts by the Woman's Christian Temperance Union and the Woman's Educational and Industrial Union. New Orleans was the only other southern city to have a police matron at that time. Hoyt, 106.
55. Clipping, Lyle Saxon papers.
56. Ibid.
57. Ibid.
58. *Memphis Commercial Appeal*, 13 February 1898.
59. Julia Bryan Grosvenor, "Flotsam," manuscript in the possession of Mrs. Niles Grosvenor, Memphis, Tenn.
60. *Memphis Commercial Appeal*, 13, 28 February 1898.
61. *Memphis News Scimitar*, 8 April, 1909.
62. Ibid. Investigation of local labor conditions by the Department of Philanthropy since the very early 1900s was probably a cumulative influence in winning a female inspector.
63. The close connection between the Nineteenth Century Club and the Board of Health was undoubtedly cemented — and may well have been initiated — by the fact that the president of that city agency, Dr. L. J. Andrews, was married to a member of the Nineteenth Century Club. This gave the women access to the government department and also provided a channel from the municipality to activist citizens.
64. Young, 274.
65. *Memphis News Scimitar*, 1 April 1909.
66. Ibid., 8 May 1909.
67. Young, 275.
68. Ibid.
69. Marcus J. Stewart and William T. Black, Jr., eds., *History of Medicine in Memphis* (Jackson, Tenn.: McCowat-Mercer Press, 1971), 60.
70. Minutes, Nineteenth Century Club, 5 August 1908, 80.
71. *22nd Annual Announcement*, Nineteenth Century Club, 1912–13, 20.
72. Clipping, scrapbook, Nineteenth Century Club. It was largely because of the efforts of Dr. Andrews that in 1907 some cottages on the river bluff were converted for use as the city's first tuberculosis hospital.

However conditions were such as to prompt descriptions of the "hospital" as a "deathtrap" and there was much agitation for an improved facility. In 1921 Oakville Sanitorium was opened. Stewart and Black, 59, 69.

73. *Woman's Work in Tennessee*, 91.

74. Among the female medical doctors in Memphis in the early twentieth century, the most is known about Dr. Elizabeth Kane. She was a very active member of the Nineteenth Century Club as well as the Tennessee Federation of Women's Clubs and was the first woman on the Memphis City Hospital Staff of Surgeons. She received her medical training at the Woman's Medical College in Baltimore and the University of Nashville, from which she graduated in 1898. Kane's name appears repeatedly in the Nineteenth Century Club minutes. She was on the Executive Board in 1910 and 1911, chaired the Health Department in 1915, and instigated a number of efforts between the club and the city's Board of Health to improve conditions in Memphis. In 1917 Kane brought Dr. Rachel Yarros of Hull House to speak to the Nineteenth Century Club on the topic of "Social Hygiene." Kane also served as Chief of Gynecology for the Associated Charities Dispensary and in 1918 offered her services to the Memphis Health Department to establish a free clinic for working girls, for which the Nineteenth Century Club offered rooms. Kane was instrumental in the formation of a group called the Medical Women's Club, which included Drs. Sara C. York and Josephine Pearl Stevens — both graduates of the University of Tennessee — and medical students Louise Beecher, Agnes Hull, and Elise Rutledge. Dr. Stevens was from Jackson, Tennessee, and after graduating from the University of Tennessee had studied in Chicago. She was a pathologist and anaesthesiologist and also worked for the Gynecology Department of the Associated Charities Dispensary. Other Memphis women in the medical professions included Dr. Bohano, a osteopath who was a graduate of the Kirkville, Missouri, School of Osteopathy and who was on the staff of the Lucy Brinkley Hospital and the Memphis City Hospital; Dr. May L. Brooks, the only female dentist in Memphis; and Drs. Alba Mead and Louise C. Drouillard. Dr. Brooks had graduated from Northwestern University and was said to be a "pioneeer in the business world of Memphis," opening the way for other women (*Club Affairs*, March 1918, 8). Dr. Mead was a member of the Nineteenth Century Club and Dr. Drouillard of the Women's Christian Association. These doctors seem to have been well integrated in the female community, but their reception as professionals by the male establishment is difficult to assess. Dr. Bohano said she had found "no prejudice

against her from men in medicine" (*Club Affairs*, March 1916, 8). However, although both she and Elizabeth Kane were on the staff of the city hospital, there is no mention of them by medical men and they do not appear in Stewart and Black's *History of Medicine in Memphis.* There is a great need for research on women and medicine in Memphis.

75. *Club Affairs,* March 1916, 8.
76. *22nd Annual Announcement,* Nineteenth Century Club, 1912–13, 20.
77. Mrs. DeLoach's husband, Josiah, had been a pioneer in Memphis. He became a large cotton planter and was a prominent name in the business world throughout the lower Mississippi valley.
78. Clipping, scrapbook, Nineteenth Century Club.
79. *Public Acts of Tennessee,* 1915, 38.
80. *Woman's Work in Tennessee,* 77–78.
81. Elizabeth Saxon, for example, was a member of the Nineteenth Century Club and in 1897 to 1898 was listed as chair of the Committee on History and Philosophy. Elise Selden and Grace Smith are also examples of women who were prominent within the Nineteenth Century Club, and both were also founding members of the Memphis Equal Rights Association. Smith was the association's first vice-president, and in 1900 Selden succeeded Lide Meriwether as president of the Tennessee Equal Suffrage Association. *Yearbook,* 1897–98, Nineteenth Century Club; *Memphis Daily Appeal,* 28 May 1889; Prescott, 94.
82. *Memphis Appeal-Avalanche,* 17 November 1892.
83. Minutes, Nineteenth Century Club, 1906–14, *passim.*
84. Minutes, Nineteenth Century Club, 2 January 1918, 64.
85. Among the leaders in Nashville were Mrs. M. M. Betts; Mrs. Isaac Reese, a former president of the Nineteenth Century Club; Mrs. Alex Y. Scott, whose speech before the Tennessee legislature was given much credit for swaying opinion; Mrs. Harry B. Anderson; Mrs. A. B. Pittman, and Mrs. R. B. Buchanan.
86. The founders were Jenny Higbee, Louise Selden, Mrs. W. H. Bates, Mrs. Jerome Baxter, Mrs. R. M. Drake, Mrs. C. F. Walworth, and Mrs. M. E. Abernathy. *Memphis Appeal-Avalanche,* 17 November 1890.
87. *The Gleaner,* May 1892, 104.
88. *Memphis Commercial Appeal,* 31 March 1913.
89. *Memphis Press Scimitar,* 24 September 1956.
90. Ibid., 29 April 1909.
91. Otis Jones, *Memphis State University, First Half Century 1912–1962* (Memphis, 1970), 91.
92. Women received the right to hold the office of Superintendent of Education in 1889. *Public Acts of Tennessee,* 1889, 213; *Memphis Daily Appeal,* 1 April 1889, 4. Messick was a graduate at the Uni-

versity of Chicago. She had read that a new coeducational university had been established in Chicago and in 1892 traveled there in search of it. It proved difficult to find, and she related being "beset with fears" as the cab left the city behind in the search. Stopping at a drugstore for directions, she learned of a man named Harper whom she was told had started a new school. This turned out to be Dr. William Rainey Harper, president of the University of Chicago. Harper took Messick to a hotel where new faculty members were staying, and there she remained with Miss Marion Talbot, Dean of Women. The faculty named Messick "The Original Aborigine"—the earliest graduates being called "The Aborigines." *Memphis Press Scimitar,* 29 June 1951.

93. 16th Annual Announcement, Nineteenth Century Club, 1906–7, 9. The committee members included Messick, Suzanne Scruggs, Mrs. J. Wesley Halliburton, Mrs. Malcolm R. Patterson, and Mrs. Percy Finley. Scruggs was chairman of the Nineteenth Century Club's Education Department at the time and had almost singlehandedly initiated the playground movement in Memphis, as well as establishing the Juvenile Court. See ch. 5.

94. These women were Mabel Williams; Lillian Johnson; Mrs. Charles B. Bryan, president of the Nineteenth Century Club; Mrs. Earle Harris, from the general membership; Suzanne Scruggs, who officially represented the Public School Association but who had also been a member of the Nineteenth Century Club; and Mrs. Mamie Cain, representing the Memphis Teachers League.

95. *Memphis Commercial Appeal,* 16 June 1909.

96. Jones, 89.

97. Minutes, Nineteenth Century Club, 10 June 1910.

98. *12th Annual Announcement,* Nineteenth Century Club, 1902–3.

99. *13th Annual Announcement,* Nineteenth Century Club, 1903–4.

100. Minutes, Nineteenth Century Club, 16 January 1907.

101. In 1919 the Elizabeth Club was opened at 360 Carroll Street as a boarding residence for young working women, the work of the Girls' Welfare Committee of the Nineteenth Century Club. Mr. Joseph Newberger, the husband of a member, had volunteered to guarantee the purchase and financing by donations from businessmen in the community. The Elizabeth Club was a separate institution, but the Nineteenth Century Club appointed two-thirds of the Elizabeth Club's board, with the president selected from that group. Minutes, Nineteenth Century Club, 1 January 1919; 2 July 1919. In November 1920, Mrs. Celia Lowenstein Samelson, a Nineteenth Century Club member, gave a residence at 756 Jefferson Street, to be a trusteeship of the Nineteenth Century Club. It, too, served as a

residence for working girls. It was called the Elias Lowenstein Club in honor of Celia Samelson's father, and had the same board of directors as the Elizabeth Club. By 1925 approximately one hundred girls were accommodated by the two residences. *75th the Anniversary Volume,* Nineteenth Century Club, 1890–1965.

102. Minutes, Nineteenth Century Club, 6 April 1910.
103. Ibid., 8 July 1910.
104. Ibid., 10 June 1910; 5 February 1913; 5 July 1916; 14 September 1917; 5 June 1918.
105. *Memphis Commercial Appeal,* 30 March 1905.
106. Clipping, scrapbook, Nineteenth Century Club.
107. "Confidential Memorandum Dealing with the Nineteenth Century Club of Memphis, Tennessee," Nineteenth Century Club, Memphis, Tenn.
108. Ibid.

Chapter 5. Suzanne Conlan Scruggs

1. Scruggs was born in 1862 and educated in the Boston public school system. She frequently returned to New England for summer vacations. Scruggs often compared Memphis to Boston, finding much in her native city that she wished to see emulated in her adopted southern city. Her idea for a public school association in Memphis, for example, was based on the Boston association. See Woman's Public School Association, Articles and Reports File, box 5, Scruggs papers, Memphis Room, Memphis Public Library, hereinafter cited as Scruggs papers.
2. Scruggs was also the Nineteenth Century Club's first corresponding secretary and served as chair of the Education Department in 1906 to 1907.
3. Scruggs had six children, four of whom survived into adulthood.
4. Miscellaneous papers, Woman's Public School Association File, box 5, Scruggs papers.
5. School Lunch Program File, box 5, Scruggs papers.
6. Woman's Public School Association, Articles and Reports File, box 5, Scruggs papers.
7. Scruggs was an inveterate letter-writer. Her papers are full of correspondence from numerous reform organizations which she consulted in planning her campaigns in Memphis.
8. Scruggs and C. P. J. Mooney, editor of the *Memphis Commercial Appeal,* lived in the same neighborhood, and it appears she had gotten the editor's attention when working on organizing the Playground Associa-

tion. Letter to Mrs. Thomas Scruggs from C. P. J. Mooney, 16 September 1908, Correspondence, Playground Association File, box 4, Scruggs papers.

9. Woman's Public School Association, Articles and Reports File, box 5, Scruggs papers.

10. Some of the clubs involved were the Housekeepers' Club, Nineteenth Century Club, Woman's Club, Salon Circle, Talkitanti Circle, Germania Club, Memphis Press and Author's Club, and the Beethoven Club.

11. *Memphis Commercial Appeal,* 3 June 1905.

12. Ibid.

13. Woman's Public School Association, Articles and Reports File, box 5, Scruggs papers.

14. *Memphis Commercial Appeal,* 3 June 1905.

15. Ibid.

16. Wharton Jones was assistant superintendent of the Memphis public schools in 1902 to 1911, and superintendent in 1911 to 1912 and 1918 to 1919. His wife was president of the Nineteenth Century Club in 1902.

17. Woman's Public School Association, Articles and Reports File, box 5, Scruggs papers; clipping, 8 February 1907, box 2, Scruggs papers.

18. Public Schools File, box 5, Scruggs papers.

19. Woman's Public School Association, Articles and Reports File, box 5, Scruggs papers.

20. Among those identified as "antis" were the assistant superintendent's wife, Mrs. Wharton Jones, and the wives of two judges, Mrs. J. M. Greer and Mrs. F. H. Heiskell. Wharton Jones later became superintendent after several unsuccessful tries for the job. The superintendent at the time of Scruggs's report, General George Gordon, was elected to the United States Congress in 1906. What political ambitions Greer and Heiskell may have had were never explained, but as part of the city administration, their wives may have been acting out of concern for bad publicity to the city generally.

21. Club minutes reveal only that Scruggs disagreed with the governing board's interpretation that her dues during a certain period were delinquent, and apparently she refused to pay them. In December 1908, a resolution was adopted by the club's governing board declaring Scruggs in default and that she was not to be regarded as a member of the club. Scruggs raised the issue again in 1915, but neither side changed its position. Scruggs is not listed as a member after 1908. See Minutes, Nineteenth Century Club, 7, 21 October, 2 November, 3 December 1908; 3 February, 7 April 1915.

22. *Memphis Commercial Appeal,* 1 July 1905.

23. Other committees were: Industrial Education, High Schools, Conferences with the Board of Education, Medical Inspection of the Schools, Membership, Aid to Teachers, Libraries, and Finance.
24. Clipping, "Letter to the Editor," 7 July 1909, box 5, Scruggs papers.
25. Ibid.
26. While Scruggs had taken it upon herself to speak on behalf of the "masses," her work did not go unnoticed among that segment of the population, and the response she received from them was that of encouragement. See Public School Correspondence File, box 3, Scruggs papers.
27. One example of the more testy responses came from Chairman Malone in 1909. Upon being asked to make an accounting of the board's receipts and expenditures for the last three years, he was reported to have remarked that if the request were repeated he would tell the legislative council to "go to the devil." Letter to Mr. A. B. Hill, secretary of the Board of Education, from Ennis M. Douglas, city register, Public School Correspondence File, box 3, Scruggs papers.
28. *Memphis Commercial Appeal*, 1, 3 July 1905.
29. They pointed out that thirty-three girls and seven boys had received diplomas in 1905.
30. If private school attendance was added, the figure still only reached 33 percent. Woman's Public School Association, Articles and Reports File, box 5, Scruggs papers; *Memphis Commercial Appeal*, 4 January, 16 July 1905.
31. Woman's Public School Association, Articles and Reports File, Box 5, Scruggs Papers.
32. *Memphis Commercial Appeal*, 11 April 1905.
33. Ibid., 15 September 1905.
34. Ibid., 10 September 1905.
35. Ibid., 11 January 1910.
36. Ibid.
37. Ibid., 10 April 1906.
38. Ibid., 15 September 1905.
39. Several very influential men were involved, many of them doctors: Dr. Max Goltman (later president of the Board of Health), Dr. Marcus Haase, Dr. B. G. Henning, Dr. Louis Leroy, Dr. J. L. Minor, Dr. B. F. Turner, and Dr. E. C. Ellett. Also businessmen: A. S. Caldwell, J. M. Goodbar, Robert Galloway, E. B. LeMaster, and M. B. Trezevant. Some prominent clergymen were: Rev. William Neel, Rev. James M. Winchester, and Rabbi M. Samfield.
40. Clipping, 7 January 1908, Public Education Association File, box 5, Scruggs papers. Elizabeth Messick was County Superintendent of Public Instruction.

41. *Memphis Commercial Appeal*, 18 August 1907.
42. Ibid., 5 September 1908.
43. "For a Better Memphis," Playground Association File, box 4, Scruggs papers.
44. Ibid.
45. Ibid.
46. Clipping, Playground Association File, box 4, Scruggs papers.
47. Playground Association, Bayou Articles File, box 4, Scruggs papers. After Scruggs succeeded in getting the playgrounds established in Memphis, she introduced the idea of a "Playground Police." She organized groups of boys who had previously been leaders of gangs and gave them the responsibility for keeping order. She believed this was a good experience in democracy.
48. *Memphis Commercial Appeal*, 14 March 1908.
49. Ibid.
50. Ibid.
51. Playground Association, Bayou Articles File, box 4, Scruggs papers.
52. Some of the incorporators were: E. H. Crump, Miss Marion Griffin, Attorney General Z. N. Estes, and Henry Craft. Some honorary incorporators were Bishop Thomas Gailor, Rev. Joseph R. Hefferman, Rabbi M. Samfield, Dr. Heber Jones, and Miss Elizabeth Messick.
53. *Memphis Press Scimitar*, 12 May 1910.
54. Third Annual Report, Associated Charities, 1913–14, 3.
55. *Memphis Commercial Appeal*, 18 July 1915.
56. Ibid.
57. Scruggs used Lindsey's ideas as a guide in organizing the juvenile court in Memphis. Lindsey, in turn, complimented Scruggs's efforts and urged her not to become discouraged. See Juvenile Court Correspondence File, box 3, Scruggs papers.
58. Miller, 106–8.
59. Leroy Leflore, Eugene N. Turner, and John C. Jones, "A History of the Juvenile Court of Memphis and Shelby County" (Paper at Southern Illinois University, Summer 1980), 237.
60. *Woman's Work in Tennessee*, 165.
61. It has been suggested that the change in the bill from county to city jurisdiction, making the new judge a city court judge with all other city functions attached, was engineered by Mayor Crump. This change would make the judge the mayor's appointee. Leflore, et al., 15–16.
62. Manuscript, Juvenile Court File, box 3, Scruggs papers.
63. Ibid.
64. Letter to Hon. Ben Hooper from Mrs. Thomas Scruggs, 1 April 1913, Juvenile Court File, box 3, Scruggs papers.
65. Manuscript, Juvenile Court File, box 3, Scruggs papers.

66. Clipping, 29 December 1910, Juvenile Court File, box 3, Scruggs papers.
67. Initial members included the Young Men's Christian Association, Playground Association, Workingmen's Civic League, Knights of Columbus, Women's Christian Temperance Union, King's Daughters of the Needy Circle, and the Trades and Labor Council.
68. Clipping, 29 December 1910, Juvenile Court File, box 3, Scruggs papers.
69. See Children's Protective Union, Correspondence 1910–13 File, box 5, Scruggs papers.
70. Clipping, 29 December 1910, Juvenile Court File, box 3, Scruggs papers.
71. Ibid.
72. Ibid.
73. Ibid.
74. See School Lunch Program File, box 5, Scruggs papers.
75. "Minutes of the Third Annual State Congress on the Welfare of the Child under the Auspices of the Tennessee Congress of Mothers and Parent-Teacher Associations," 27, 28 March 1914, Knoxville, Tenn., Tennessee Congress of Mothers, Correspondence and Articles File, box 6, Scruggs papers.
76. Tennessee was divided into three sections — East, Middle, and West — with a vice-president for each.
77. Tennessee Congress of Mothers File, box 6, Scruggs papers.
78. Ibid.
79. *Memphis Commercial Appeal*, 8 March 1911.
80. Ibid.
81. Clipping, 9 March 1911, Tennessee Congress of Mothers File, box 6, Scruggs papers.
82. *Memphis Commercial Appeal*, 8 March 1911.
83. The committee was composed of citizens and three city commissioners.
84. *Memphis Commercial Appeal*, 24 March 1911.
85. Clipping, 25 March 1911, Tennessee Congress of Mothers File, box 6, Scruggs papers.
86. Clipping, 25 March 1913, Public Schools File, box 3, Scruggs papers.
87. *Memphis Commercial Appeal*, 9 June 1914. By 1913 political factionalism was another element that stirred animosities, and the five-man school board had split into procity administration and anticity administration factions. Scruggs had long been an opponent of "politics" on the board in the belief that these considerations took precedence over what was good for the children.
88. *Memphis Commercial Appeal*, 9 June 1914.
89. *Memphis Commercial Appeal*, 9 October 1916.
90. It has also been suggested that she was not in perfect health, although the nature of her ailments is not known. She lived until 1945.

Interview, Mrs. Elizabeth Goodheart, daughter of Suzanne Scruggs, 25 April 1986, Memphis, Tenn.

Conclusion

1. Clipping, Turner family scrapbook, in the possession of Mrs. Carroll Turner, Memphis, Tenn.
2. *Club Affairs*, November 1915, 16.
3. Smith-Rosenberg.
4. *Club Affairs*, March 1916, 6.

Bibliography

Books

Beard, Mattie Duncan. *The W.C.T.U. in the Volunteer State*. Kingsport, Tenn.: Kingsport Press, Inc., 1962.

Berg, Barbara J. *The Remembered Gate: Origins of American Feminism*. New York: Oxford University Press, 1978.

Blair, Karen. *The Clubwoman as Feminist*. New York: Holmes and Meier, 1980.

Bordin, Ruth. *Woman and Temperance: The Quest for Power and Liberty, 1873–1900*. Philadelphia: Temple University Press, 1981.

Brownell, Blaine and David R. Goldfield, eds. *The City in Southern History*. Port Washington, N.Y.: Kennikat Press, 1977.

Capers, Gerald M. *Biography of a River Town*. Chapel Hill: University of North Carolina Press, 1939.

Commercial and Statistical Review of the City of Memphis, Tennessee. N.p., Reilly & Thomas, 1883.

Connelly, Mark David. *The Response to Prostitution in the Progressive Era*. Chapel Hill: University of North Carolina Press, 1980.

Conway, Clara. *Letters and Lyrics*. N.p., privately printed, 1905.

———. *Silver-Lined Days; Leaves from a Notebook of Old-World Travel*. Memphis: Paul & Douglas, 1902.

Coppock, Paul. *Memphis Sketches*. Friends of Memphis and Shelby County Libraries, 1976.

Cott, Nancy. *The Bonds of Womanhood: "Woman's Sphere" in New England 1790–1835*. New Haven: Yale University Press, 1978.

Croly, Jane Cunningham. *Sorosis: Its Origins and History*. New York: J. J. Little, 1886. Repr., New York: Arno Press, 1975.

D'Arusmont, Frances Wright. *Views of Society and Manners in America*. Edited by Paul R. Baker. Cambridge, Mass.: Harvard University Press, 1963.

Davies-Rodgers, Ellen. *The Great Book, Calvary Protestant Episcopal Church 1832–1972*. Memphis: The Plantation Press, 1973.

Davis, James D. *The History of the City of Memphis*. Memphis: Hite, Crumpton & Kelly, Printers, 1873; facsimile edition, West Tennessee Historical Society, 1972.

Davis, John H. *St. Mary's Cathedral, 1858–1958*. Memphis: Chapter of St. Mary's Cathedral, 1958.

Dykeman, Wilma. *Tennessee Women, Past and Present*. Memphis: Tennessee Commission for the Humanities, 1977.

Eckhardt, Celia Morris. *Fanny Wright, Rebel in America*. Cambridge, Mass.: Harvard University Press, 1984.

Epstein, Barbara L. *The Politics of Domesticity: Women, Evangelism, and Temperance in Nineteenth Century America*. Middletown, Conn.: Wesleyan University Press, 1981.

Fairbank, A. W. (Mrs.), ed., *Emma Willard and Her Pupils or Fifty Years of Troy Female Seminary, 1822–1872*. New York: Mrs. Russell Sage, 1898.

Friedman, Jean, *The Enclosed Garden: Women and Community in the Evangelical South 1830–1900*. Chapel Hill: University of North Carolina Press, 1985.

Gilchrist, Annie. *Some Representative Women of Tennessee*. Nashville: McQuiddy Printing, 1902.

Gillum, James L. *Prominent Tennesseeans, 1796–1938*. Lewisburg, Tenn.: Who's Who Publishing Co., 1940.

Goodspeed's History of Hamilton, Knox, and Shelby Counties of Tennessee. Nashville: Goodspeed Publishing Co., 1887. Repr., Nashville: Charles and Randy Eller, 1974.

Gordon, Anna. *The Life of Frances Willard*. Evanston, Ill.: National Woman's Christian Temperance Union Publishing House, 1912.

Gordon, Elizabeth Putnam. *Women Torch Bearers*. Evanston, Ill.: National Woman's Christian Temperance Union Publishing House, 1924.

Hall, Jacquelyn Dowd. *Revolt against Chivalry*. New York: Columbia University Press, 1979.

Hamer, Philip M. *Tennessee, A History, 1673–1932*. 4 vols. New York: The American Historical Society, 1933.

Hardesty, Nancy A. *Women Called to Witness*. Nashville: Abingdon Press, 1984.

Holli, Melvin. *Reform in Detroit: Hazen S. Pingree and Urban Politics*. New York: Oxford University Press, 1969.

Hopkins, Anson Smith. *Reminiscences of an Octogenarian*. New Haven: Tuttle, Morehouse & Taylor, 1937.

Isaac, Paul. *Prohibition and Politics: Turbulent Decades in Tennessee, 1885-1920*. Knoxville: University of Tennessee Press, 1965.

Jones, Bessie Z., ed. *Hospital Sketches.* Cambridge Mass.: Harvard University Press, Belknap Press, 1960.

Kearney, Belle. *A Slaveholder's Daughter.* New York: The Abbey Press, 1900.

Keating, J. M. *History of the City of Memphis and Shelby County, Tennessee.* 2 vols. Vol. 2 edited by O. F. Vedder. Syracuse, N.Y.: D Mason & Co., 1888.

Kessler-Harris, Alice. *Women Have Always Worked.* Old Westbury, N.Y.: The Feminist Press, 1981.

Leach, William. *True Love and Perfect Union: The Feminist Reform of Sex and Society.* New York: Basic Books, 1980.

Lebsock, Suzanne. *The Free Women of Petersburg: Status and Culture in a Southern Town, 1784–1860.* New York: W. W. Norton, 1984.

Long, N. M. *Sermons and Addresses.* Memphis: S. C. Toof, 1906.

Massey, Mary Elizabeth. *Bonnet Brigades.* New York: Alfred A. Knopf, 1966.

———. *Ersatz in the Confederacy.* Columbia: University of South Carolina Press, 1952.

———. *Refugee Life in the Confederacy.* Baton Rouge: Louisiana State University Press, 1964.

Matthews, Donald G. *Religion in the Old South.* Chicago: University of Chicago Press, 1977.

McDonald, Harriett I., comp. *Memphis Sunshine.* Memphis, 1903.

McFarland, L. B. *Memoirs and Addresses,* n.p., n.d.

McIlwaine, Shields. *Memphis Down in Dixie.* New York: E. P. Dutton, 1948.

Memphis Press and Author's Club. *The Sketch Book.* Springfield, Mo.: Jewell Publishing Co., 1907.

The Memphis Society Blue Book. New York: Dau Publishing Co., 1900.

Meriwether, Elizabeth Avery. *Recollections of 92 years: 1824–1916.* Nashville: The Tennessee Historical Commission, 1958.

Meriwether, Lide. *Soundings.* Memphis: Boyle & Chapman, 1972.

Miller, William D. *Memphis during the Progressive Era, 1900–1917.* Memphis: Memphis State University Press, 1975.

Moore, John Trotwood. *Tennessee, the Volunteer State, 1769–1923.* 3 vols. Chicago: S. J. Clarke, 1923.

Raine, Julia. *Law in Tennessee.* n.p., 1910.

———. *In Nineteen-Ten. A Protest against Conditions of Tennessee.* n.p., 1910.

Riley, Glenda. *Women and Indians on the Frontier.* Albuquerque: University of New Mexico Press, 1984.

Roper, James. *The Founding of Memphis, 1818–1820.* Memphis: The Memphis Sesquicentennial, 1970.

Ryan, Mary P. *Cradle of the Middle Class: The Family in Onedia County, New York, 1790–1865.* Cambridge: Cambridge University Press, 1981.

————. *Womanhood in America.* New York: New Viewpoints, 1975.

Saxon, Elizabeth Lyle. *A Southern Woman's War Time Reminiscences.* Memphis: Press of the Pilcher Printing Co., 1905.

————. *Poems of Elizabeth Lyle Saxon.* Dallas: Clyde C. Cockrell Co., 1932.

Scott, Anne Firor. *Making the Invisible Woman Visible.* Urbana: University of Illinois Press, 1984.

————. *The Southern Lady, from Pedestal to Politics, 1830–1930.* Chicago: University of Chicago Press, 1970.

Sklar, Kathryn Kish. *Catharine Beecher: A Study in American Domesticity.* New York: W. W. Norton, 1973.

Smith, S. E. D. (Mrs.) *The Soldier's Friend.* Memphis: The Bulletin Publishing Co., 1867.

Social Register of Memphis 1925. Memphis: Penn-Renshaw [1925].

Speer, William S. *Sketches of Prominent Tennesseans.* Nashville: Elbert B. Tavel, 1888.

Stanton, Elizabeth Cady, Susan B. Anthony, and Matilda Joslyn Gage, eds. *History of Woman Suffrage.* 6 vols. New York: Arno & The New York Times, 1969.

Stewart, Marcus J., and William T. Black, eds. *History of Medicine in Memphis.* Jackson, Tenn.: McCowat-Mercer Press, 1971.

Tatum, Noreen Dunn. *A Crown of Service: A Story of Woman's Work in the Methodist Episcopal Church, South, from 1878–1940.* Nashville: Parthenon Press, 1960.

Taylor, A. Elizabeth. *The Woman Suffrage Movement in Tennessee.* New York: Bookman Associates, 1957.

Trollope, Frances M. *Domestic Manners of the Americans.* With an introduction by James E. Mooney. Barre, Mass.: Imprint Society, 1969.

Willard, Frances. *Woman and Temperance or, The Work and Workers of the Woman's Christian Temperance Union.* New York: Arno Press, 1972.

Willard, Frances, and Mary A. Livermore, eds. *A Woman of the Century.* Buffalo: Charles Wells Moulton, 1893. Repr., Detroit: Gale Research Co., 1967.

Williamson, Joel. *The Crucible of Race.* New York: Oxford University Press, 1984.

Wingfield, Marshall. *Literary Memphis.* Memphis: West Tennessee Historical Society, 1942.

Woman's Work In Tennessee. Memphis: Printed under the auspices of the Tennessee Federation of Women's Clubs by Jones-Briggs Co., 1916.

Young, J. P. *Standard History of Memphis, Tennessee.* Knoxville: H. W. Crew and Co., 1912.

Articles and Unpublished Materials

Allen, J. D. (Mrs.) "Retrospection." Memphis Pink Palace Collection, Memphis Pink Palace Museum, Memphis, Tenn.

Baker, Thomas H. "The Early Newspapers of Memphis, Tennessee, 1827–1860." *West Tennessee Historical Society Papers* 17 (1963): 20–46.

Baughn, Milton L. "Social Views Reflected in Official Publications of the Cumberland Presbyterian Church 1875–1900." Ph.D. dissertation, Vanderbilt University, 1954.

Berkeley, Kathleen Christine. "Elizabeth Avery Meriwether, 'An Advocate for Her Sex': Feminism and Conservatism in the Post-Civil War South." *Tennessee Historical Quarterly* 43 (Winter 1984): 390–406.

———. "'Like a Plague of Locust': Immigration and Social Change in Memphis, Tennessee, 1850–1880." Ph.D. dissertation, University of California, Los Angeles, 1980.

———. "'The Ladies Want to Bring About Reform in the Public Schools': Public Education and Women's Rights in the Post-Civil War South." *History of Educational Quarterly* 24 (Spring 1984): 45–58.

Burt, Jesse C., Jr. "Anna Russell Cole: a Case Study of a Grande Dame." *Tennessee Historical Quarterly* 13 (1954): 127–55.

"Confidential Memorandum Dealing with the Nineteenth Century Club of Memphis, Tennessee." Nineteenth Century Club, Memphis, Tenn.

Davis, Natalie Z. "Women's History in Transition: The European Case." *Feminist Studies* 3 (Spring–Summer 1976): 83–90.

Doak, H. M. "The Development of Education in Tennessee." *American Historical Magazine* 8 (January 1903): 64–90.

Durham, Louise. "The Old Market Street School, 1870–1920." *West Tennessee Historical Society Papers* 7 (1953): 57–71.

Esgar, Mildred. "Women Involved in the Real World: a History of the Young Women's Christian Association of Cleveland, Ohio, 1868–1968." Cleveland: Western Reserve Historical Society, n.d.

Evans, Phoebe Grosvenor. "The Memphis Woman's Club 1890–1962." Memphis Room, Memphis Public Library, Memphis, Tenn.

Frazer, Leigh. "A Demographic Analysis of Memphis and Shelby County, Tennessee, 1820–1972." M. A. thesis, Memphis State University, 1972.

Grosvenor, Julia Bryan. "Flotsam." Typescript in possession of Mrs. Niles Grosvenor III, Memphis, Tenn.

———. *Genes.* Privately printed, 1982. In the possession of Mrs. Niles Grosvenor III, Memphis, Tenn.

Hammond, Lily H. "Southern Women and Racial Adjustment." Occasional papers, No. 19. Charlottesville, Va. The Trustees of the John F. Slater Fund, 1920.

Harris, Katherine. "Feminism and Temperance Reform in the Boulder WCTU." *Frontiers* 4 (Fall 1979): 19–24.

Harvey, Cathy C. "Lyle Saxon: A Portrait in Letters, 1917–1945." Ph.D. dissertation, Tulane University, 1980.

Hilliard, David Moss. "The Development of Public Education in Memphis, Tennessee, 1848–1945." Ph.D. dissertation, University of Chicago, 1946.

Hoyt, Elizabeth S. "Some Phases of the History of the Woman's Movement in Tennessee." M. A. Thesis, University of Tennessee, 1931.

Huhn, Hugh Higbee. *Biographical Notes, A Scrapbook.* Memphis Room, Memphis Public Library, Memphis, Tenn.

Jarzombek, Michelle. "The Memphis-South Memphis Conflict, 1826–1850." *Tennessee Historical Quarterly* 41 (Spring 1962): 23–36.

Johnson, R. W. "Geographic Influences in the Location and Growth of the City of Memphis." *Journal of Geography* 27 (March 1928): 85–97.

Jones, Otis. *Memphis State University, First Half Century 1912–1962.* Memphis: 1970.

Jordan, Robert H. (Mrs.) "Memphis Woman's Club." In the possession of Mrs. Niles Grosvenor III, Memphis, Tenn.

Kessler-Harris. "Women's History on Trial." *The Nation* 7 September 1985, 161.

Layman, Edith Belle. "Tennessee's Action on the Proposed Amendments to the Constitution of the United States." M. A. thesis, University of Tennessee, 1934.

Leab, Grace. "The Temperance Movement in Tennessee, 1860–1909." M. A. thesis, University of Tennessee, 1938.

Leflore, Leroy, Eugene N. Turner, and John C. Jones. "A History of the Juvenile Court of Memphis and Shelby County." Carbondale, Ill.: Center for the Study of Crime, Deliquency and Corrections, Southern Illinois University, 1980.

Leloudis, James L. "School Reform in the New South: The Women's Association for the Betterment of Public School Houses in North Carolina, 1902–1919." *Journal of American History* 69 (March 1983): 886–909.

Lerner, Gerda. "New Approaches to the Study of Women in American History." *Journal of Social History* 3 (Fall 1969): 53–69.

"Letter from Miss Anita Williams, President of Tennessee League of Women Voters to Mrs. J. D. Allen, Memphis." 24 March 1928. Memphis Pink Palace Collection, Memphis Pink Palace Museum, Memphis, Tenn.

Lewis, Virginia E. "Fifty Years of Politics in Memphis." Ph.D. dissertation. New York University, 1955.

Lyle, Mary Willett. "Early Settlement of Memphis, Recollections of Mary Willett Lyle." Memphis Historical Society Papers, ESM 4, January 1917.

Mason, Tim. "Women in Germany, 1925–1940: Family, Welfare and Work." *History Workshop* 2 (Autumn 1976): 5–32.

McIntyre, Florence M. "The History of Art in Memphis." *West Tennessee Historical Society Papers* 8 (1953): 79–92.

Melder, Keith. "Ladies Bountiful." *New York History* 48 (July 1967): 231–54.

Memphis Scrapbook, 1877–1951. West Tennessee Historical Society Miscellaneous manuscripts, No. 37. Mississippi Valley Collection, Memphis State University, Memphis, Tenn.

Mendenhall, Marjorie Stratford. "Southern Women of a 'Lost Generation.'" *South Atlantic Quarterly* 33 (October 1934): 334–53.

Meriwether, Lee. "Recollections of Memphis." *West Tennessee Historical Society Papers* 3 (1949): 90–109.

Modey, Yao Foli. "The Struggle over Prohibition in Memphis, 1880–1930." Ph.D. dissertation, Memphis State University, 1983.

Morton, Marian J. "Temperance, Benevolence and the City: The Cleveland Non-Partisan Woman's Christian Temperance Union, 1874–1900." *Ohio History* 91 (1982): 58–73.

"Nineteenth Century Club—State Convention." Memphis, 1929.

Parks, Joseph. "A Confederate Trade Center under Federal Occupation: Memphis 1862–1865." *Journal of Southern History* 7 (August 1941): 289–314.

Pearl, Ethel. "The Atrophied Rib: Urban Middle-Class Women in Jacksonian America." Ph.D. dissertation, University of Pittsburgh, 1970.

Petry, Frances C. "Memphis Women in Business, 1850–1931." Memphis, 1975. Memphis Room, Memphis Public Library, Memphis, Tenn.

Pool, Charles, Sam Shankman, and Annie Mayhew Fitzpatrick. "Three views of Old Higbee School." *West Tennessee Historical Society Papers* 20 (1966): 46–60.

Potter, David. "American Women and the American Character," in Don E. Fehrenbacher, ed., *History and American Society: Essays of David E. Potter.* New York: Oxford University Press, 1973, 277–304.

Prescott, Grace Elizabeth. "The Woman Suffrage Movement in Memphis: Its Place in the State, Sectional and National Movements." *West Tennessee Historical Society Papers* 18 (1964): 87–106.

Price, Margaret Nell. "The Development of Leadership by Southern Women through Clubs and Organizations." M. A. thesis, University of North Carolina, 1945.

Roper, James. "The Earliest Pictures of Memphis: Charles Lesuer's Drawings, 1820–1830." *West Tennessee Historical Society Papers* 25 (1971): 5–25.

———. "Marcus Winchester and the Earliest Years of Memphis." *Tennessee Historical Quarterly* 21 (1962): 326–51.

Ruegamer, Lana. "The Paradise of Exceptional Women: Chicago Women Reformers, 1863–1893." Ph.D. dissertation, Indiana University, 1982.

Ruoff, John Carl. "Southern Womanhood, 1865–1920: An Intellectual and Cultural Study." Ph.D. dissertation, University of Illinois, 1976.

Rupp, Lelia J. "Reflections on Twentieth Century America Women's History." *Reviews in American History* 9 (June 1981): 275–84.

Ryan, Mary P., "The Power of Women's Networks: A Case Study of Female Moral Reform in Antebellum America." *Feminist Studies* 5 (Spring 1979): 66–85.

Scott, Anne Firor. "Women, Religion and Social Change in the South, 1830–1930," in *Religion and the Solid South*. Edited by Samuel S. Hill. Nashville: Abingdon Press, 1972.

Smith-Rosenberg, Carroll. "The Female World of Love and Ritual: Relations between Women in Nineteenth Century America." *Signs* 1 (Autumn 1975): 1–29.

Soden, Dale E. "The Social Gospel in Tennessee: Mark Allison Matthews." *Tennessee Historical Quarterly* 41 (Summer 1982): 159–70.

"Souvenir," Twentieth Annual Congress of the Association for the Advancement of Women. Memphis, Tenn., 1892.

Stone, Lee Alexander. "Feminism." Memphis Linotype Printing Co., 1915.

Taylor, A. Elizabeth. "A Short History of the Women Suffrage Movement in Tennessee." *Tennessee Historical Quarterly* 11 (March–December 1943): 195–215.

Thompson, Edwin Bruce. "Humanitarian Reforms in Tennessee, 1820–1850." M. A. thesis, Vanderbilt University, 1935.

Tilly, Bette Baird. "Aspects of Social and Economic Life in West Tennessee before the Civil War." Ph.D. dissertation, Memphis State University, 1974.

Tracy, Sterling. "The Immigrant Population of Memphis." *West Tennessee Historical Society Papers* 4 (1950): 72–82.

Turner, B. F. (Mrs.) "Pages from the Memoirs of Mrs. B. F. Turner." 4 vols. Privately printed, 1952. In the possession of Mrs. Carroll Turner, Memphis, Tenn.

Turner family scrapbook. In the possession of Mrs. Carroll Turner, Memphis, Tenn.

Watson, Annah Robinson. "Development of the Club Idea in Memphis." *Mid-Continent Magazine* 6 (1985): 151–54.

Wingfield, Marie Gregson. "Memphis as Seen through Meriwether's Weekly." *West Tennessee Historical Society Papers* 5 (1951): 31–61.

Wooten, Fred T., Jr. "Religious Activity in Civil War Memphis." *West Tennessee Historical Quarterly* 3 (March–December 1944): 131–49.

Wrenn, Lynette Boney. "The Taxing District of Shelby County: A Political and Administrative History of Memphis, Tennessee, 1879–1893." Ph.D. dissertation, Memphis State University, 1983.

Newspapers and Magazines

Art Supplement to the Greater Memphis Edition of the Evening Scimitar. April 1899.

Centennial Edition, Memphis Commercial Appeal. 1 January 1940.

Club Affairs. October 1915–November 1917. Published monthly by the Nineteenth Century Club, Memphis, Tenn.

The Gleaner. June 1891–June 1892. A publication of the Memphis Women's Christian Association.

The Issue. Official organ of the Tennessee State Temperance Alliance, Tennessee Good Templars, Woman's Christian Temperance Union. 2 September 1886; 28 July, 4 & 25 August, 15 & 22 December 1887; 19 January, 9 February, 3 May, 28 June 1888; 12 June 1890.

Memphis Commercial Appeal, 1889–1892; 1895; 1898; 1900; 1904–1914; 1915–1917; 7 April 1921; 19 March 1922; 14 October 1932; 23 November 1952; 31 October 1978.

Memphis Evening Scimitar, 1901–1902.

Memphis News Scimitar, 1908–1909; 1912; 1913.

Memphis Press Scimitar. May 1944.

Memphis Daily Avalanche, 1879–1881; 1890.

Memphis Daily Appeal. 1861–1862; 1872–1885; 1889–1892.

Memphis Appeal-Avalanche, 1891–1893.

The South Today. October 1910.

Souvenir Edition, Memphis Appeal, December 1890.

Union Signal, 5 June 1884–25 December 1890. Temperance and Prohibition papers, WCTU Series. The Michigan Historical Collections, The Ohio Historical Society, The Woman's Christian Temperance Union. Ann Arbor: University of Michigan, 1977.

"Woman's Edition," Memphis Commercial Appeal, 14 February 1895.

Public and Institutional Records

Acts of the State of Tennessee, 1889–1919.

An Abstract of the report on the public school system of Memphis, Tennessee. Department of the Interior, Bureau of Education. Bulletin No. 72. Washington: Government Printing Office, 1919.

Annual Directories of the Women's and Young Women's Christian Association, 1902–1906. Memphis, Tenn.

Annual Meeting Minutes, 1874–1910, Woman's Christian Temperance Union. Temperance and Prohibition Papers, WCTU Series. The Michigan Historical Collections, The Ohio Historical Society, The Woman's Christian Temperance Union. Ann Arbor: University of Michigan, 1977.

Annual Reports, Associated Charities, 1911–1912, 1914–1917, 1922–1923, Memphis, Tenn.

Memphis Board of Commissioners. Summary of minutes of city council, Board of Health, etc., City of Memphis, 1826–1905.

Memphis Women's Christian Association Yearbook, 1892–1893. Memphis: J. T. Lloyd and Sons Publishers, 1893.

Minute Books, Nineteenth Century Club. 1906–1922. Nineteenth Century Club, Memphis, Tenn.

Memphis Board of Education Annual Reports, 1872–1878, 1881, 1899–1911, 1914–1918.

Minute Books, 1896–1899, Woman's Christian Temperance Union, Milan, Tenn. chapter. In the possession of Mrs. Henry Haizlip, Jr., Memphis, Tenn.

Minutes of First and Second Annual Meetings of Reorganization. Tennessee Equal Suffrage Association. Memphis, 1907–1908.

Minutes of the Legislative Council, 1895–1902, Memphis-Shelby County Archives, Memphis, Tenn.

Public School Reports, Memphis, Tenn., 1908–1909, 1911–1914.

Thirty-Third Year Book, Women's and Young Women's Christian Association, 1907–1908, Memphis, Tenn.

Women's and Young Women's Christian Association History — By Laws. Memphis, 1952.

Yearbook, Women's Christian Association, 1892–1893. Memphis: J. T. Lloyd's Sons.

Yearbooks of the Memphis Woman's Club, 1955–1956, 1956–1957. In the possession of Mrs. Shepherd Tate, Memphis, Tenn.

Yearbooks/Annual Announcements, Nineteenth Century Club, 1890–1918.

Bibliographies and Guides

James, Edward T., Janet Wilson James, and Paul S. Boyer, eds. *Notable American Women, 1607–1950: A Biographical Dictionary.* 3 vols. Cambridge, Mass.: Harvard University Press Belknap Press, 1971.

Jimerson, Randal C., Francis X. Blouin, and Charles A. Isetts, eds. *Guide to the Microfilm Edition of Temperance and Prohibition Papers.* Michigan Historical Collections, The Ohio Historical Society, Woman's Christian Temperance Union. Ann Arbor: University of Michigan, 1977.

The Register of Women's Clubs. New York: Essex Publishing Co., 1933.

Who's Who in Tennessee. Memphis: Paul & Douglas Co., 1911.

Wiley, Henry C., ed. *The Biographical Cyclopaedia of American Women.* 3 vols. New York: L. Halvord & Co., 1928.

Manuscript Collections and Personal Interviews

Love Family papers. Memphis Room, Memphis Public Library, Memphis, Tenn.

Lyle Saxon papers. Department of Manuscripts, Tulane University, New Orleans, La.

Meriwether family papers. Mississippi Valley Collection, Memphis State University, Memphis, Tenn.

Walter and Myers family papers. Mississippi Valley Collection, Memphis State University, Memphis, Tenn.

Interview, Mrs. Elizabeth Goodheart, 25 April 1986, Memphis, Tenn.

Interview, Mrs. Niles Grosvenor III, 7 May 1986, Memphis, Tenn.

Interview, Mrs. C. N. Grosvenor, Jr., 15 May 1986, Memphis, Tenn.

Interview, Mrs. Henry Haizlip, 11 October 1986, Memphis, Tenn.

Interview, Mrs. Carroll Turner, 18 November 1985, Memphis, Tenn.

Index

*Elite Women and the Reform Impulse
in Memphis, 1875–1915*
was designed by Kay Jursik,
composed by Lithocraft, Inc.,
and printed by Cushing-Malloy, Inc.
This book is set in Palatino
and printed on 60 lb. Glatfelter Natural.